For: Cathy

Always Live with 'Limitless' Thinking.

A Limitless Life in a Powerless World

Be well
Be at peace!

Lisa Marie Runfola

Lisa Marie Runfola
6/14/19

BALBOA.
PRESS

A DIVISION OF HAY HOUSE

Balboa Press books may be ordered through booksellers or by contacting:

Balboa Press
A Division of Hay House
1663 Liberty Drive
Bloomington, IN 47403
www.balboapress.com
1 (877) 407-4847

Print information available on the last page.

ISBN: 978-1-9822-1959-8 (sc)
ISBN: 978-1-9822-1961-1 (hc)
ISBN: 978-1-9822-1960-4 (e)

Library of Congress Control Number: 2019900202

Balboa Press rev. date: 02/04/2019

Praise for A Limitless Life in a Powerless World

In this captivating memoir, you will laugh and cry for Lisa Marie as she journeys from the caterpillar stretching its legs on land only to find itself confined in its cocoon, and you will cheer when she breaks free becoming the butterfly with limitless potential.

—Dawn Lynn - Author, Speaker, Medium

If I took anything away from this book it is merely that families can be built out of any circumstance. Some beings have appointments with life and others have appointments with mortality, but through the good, bad, or indifferent, Lisa Marie chooses to love beyond borders, extend grace, and embrace the unknown with the most profound faith that everything can happen if you choose to simply walk through that open door. It is with so much love and respect that each detail was carefully written. I am thankful to have been able to see into a little part of this life. It is definitely one story that deserves to be told.

—Jen Soos

There are many people that come into our lives for a reason and a purpose ... some of those people are larger than life and almost 'magical' to be around. I have been blessed with more than a few of these people in my life and Lisa Marie Runfola is one of them. Her words of truth, even when raw and painful, are gifts of the heart to be shared and will resonate with those who long to not be stuck and powerless. Lisa Marie has found a way to do this with her life by taking leaps of faith ... and now with yet another 'leap of faith' ... she is graciously sharing her story in this heartfelt and moving memoir.

—Debra Rich Hamsher

To my ex-husband, Richard,
for releasing the butterfly

To my husband, Andrew,
for catching its beauty

Contents

Prologue

As the warm sunshine shone down on my face that early afternoon, I felt a ray of hope but heard a world of silence.

The green trees swayed gently in the light wind as cries of sorrow, disbelief, and remorse rose up from the mourners who came to say goodbye to their beloved son, father, nephew, uncle, friend, and husband.

While looking across the land that had once been my playground of opportunity, I felt the lost souls—those who had lived long lives and those who had been with us for only a short time.

When I was a teenager, this was the neighborhood cemetery I visited with my family and friends. Our creative adolescent minds led us to explore the grounds with a sense of wonder about the unknown.

On summer afternoons we ran through the rows of big and small graves as kids do, stopping by to read the dates and challenging our friends with the mathematics of how long this or that person had lived. The names were always so intriguing to us; we stopped when we stumbled upon an old-fashioned one, using our vivid imaginations to transform ourselves into a Florence or an Elda. We let our imaginations run wild with the wonder of what their lives had held for them.

We were sad when we found a grave site that held a picture of a child. My friends and I challenged each other to subtract a date of death from a birthdate, only to realize the person had passed away at the same age we were. This discovery brought a great sense of sadness and wonder about God and about how he had taken back the children he gave. It soon made us realize we are all gifts—gifts given with an unknown expiration, the kind of gifts that are opened each day, yielding endless possibilities. We often stood in silence with our eyes wide open and tried to imagine the lives these people had led.

But I was no longer a teenager. Here, today, I was burying my children's father.

We were all in utter shock and disbelief that this burial was taking place before our eyes and on a typical early spring day that showed the signs of the season. Surrounded by yellow daffodils, purple crocuses, and tulips trying to peek through the hard surface of the cemetery grounds, I stood with my body frozen still.

After we parked our car, I opened the door and stepped down on the semi-frozen yet slushy ground, my heart beginning to race. Why was I here? This was the place where I had come as a young teenager to find solitude, silence, a ray of hope, or an inspired idea. Just a few miles down the road stood my childhood home. I had never imagined that I would be here forty years later under such tragic circumstances.

Off in the distance, I could see a traditional white tent with a few rows of chairs beneath. As we approached the grave site and the tent beside it, it became more obvious that this wouldn't be a traditional Catholic burial. Keeping a close eye on where my children were being directed to sit, I stopped. I stood as if an invisible wall had been dropped down in front of me. I wanted to step forward but felt as if a nonexistent barrier were blocking my body. I was frozen still on the outside and shaking on the inside. My legs felt as if they were going to fall beneath me.

My longtime friend Lucille put her arm through mine on the left side, and my beautiful friend Margie pulled me up on the right side. Someone said, "Come on, you need to be with your children underneath the tent. You need to come." I stood looking at all the stone-white faces. I considered the dark-gray, subdued color under the shadow of the tent. It looked cold to me and not like a place I wanted to be. A sudden sadness and disbelief came over me as I watched the onset of others lining up in rows.

My oldest daughter, Rose, was told to sit here, and then my oldest son, Rico, was motioned to sit there, and my youngest son, Enzo, sat next to his sister. I couldn't move. I had to watch their faces.

I tried to gather up the strength to take another step forward, but my body wouldn't move past the invisible solid wall. As I looked up to the blue-gray, slightly cloudy sky, a beam of warmth began to emerge from behind the clouds. The sun began to shine warmth on my face. I knew I needed to just stand exactly where I was. I felt completely powerless. I was a mama bear coming to protect, nurture, and love her cubs at what I felt had to be the most traumatic time of their lives: The burial of their father.

Rows and rows of faces lined up behind my children. Everyone looked as if he or she were tied up in his or her own grief. I felt there wasn't anyone there to comfort them. I had full view of it all. There, in the warmth of the sunshine, I knew: Richard was with us.

That day and the days to follow were life changing. And today I can say that everything that left me powerless ended up giving me more than I could ever imagine.

My journey has changed my view of the life we are given, how we live it, and how quickly it can be taken away. My heart, usually wide open for everyone, has narrowed so I can focus on what I need to concentrate on in my immediate surroundings. Today I am more protective of myself and my children. I cherish the simple things like Friday night movie nights with them. Nothing, from their giggles to their grand life accomplishments, goes unnoticed.

This book explores the events in my life that led up to the death and burial of my ex-husband. It catalogs my journey toward embracing powerlessness and using it to become limitless.

The word *powerless* means "without ability or influence." When we are powerless, we have no ability to affect a particular situation or event occurring around us. On the day I buried my ex-husband, I was powerless. I had no ability to fix what had happened or change what was going to happen next. I could only watch it play out. None of us ask to be put in a situation where we feel powerless; nor do we feel good about it, but sometimes the world is like that.

What I did know was that this would be the last time in my life when I would allow anyone or any event to limit me. I do have a choice; we all do, always. We can choose what to do with ourselves when we find ourselves in a powerless position; we can choose to accept our powerlessness and live a limitless life anyway. To be *limitless* is not to be held back, even when we can do little to change the circumstances around us. It means to choose happiness anyway.

While you read through the chapters of this memoir, you will see that I have had choices at every step in my life. It is what I did with these choices that molded me into the person I am today. Overall, I chose to live my life with purpose. I took the unknown path many times, backed up with my faith in God. It is my hope that parts of my story will resonate with you so you, too, can face your own powerlessness without letting it limit you. My thought process is very simple: Be open to receive the gift that is bestowed on you today. Accept it with the deepest gratitude. Though it may put you in a powerless position, your limitless life is still waiting to be lived.

Throughout my life, I accumulated wounds created by heartbreak and trauma. With these wounds, my soul created its own unique pattern I see like a piece of Swiss cheese cut out with holes. I took care of everyone I could but found that my holes were left unfilled. As much as I tried to fill them with the love of others or materialistic things, the holes still remained. It turned out that I needed to first recognize that they were there and then begin to fill them myself. By practicing self-care, treating myself with kindness, and loving myself again, I slowly began the healing process. The same is true for all of us. We are all like Swiss cheese with our own individual holes. It's up to us to see them, honor them, and then take care of ourselves the best we can. This is the only way our Swiss cheese holes can be filled.

Each of us has endured some sort of life trauma. I cannot overstress the importance of self-care during our difficult times; it is essential to our well-being. During times of loss, many of us reach out and make sure everyone around us is being tended to. We often lose ourselves during that process and neglect ourselves, leaving our Swiss cheese holes open. This situation causes many other problems to creep up within us. It keeps us stuck in our powerlessness, unable to see our limitless possibilities.

My story takes you from one part of the globe across the pond to another continent. I catalog my unique life experiences, from growing up in upstate New York to becoming an expat, and from being in a traditional first marriage to adding a second husband and a second round of kids to the family. These uncommon choices have helped me to remain open to my limitless life so even when I'm powerless, I can still be happy.

Anytime I've felt really stuck—anytime it seemed like I didn't have power over anything at all—I have found that by simply rearranging my priorities, I have been able to make an internal change and create an external result. In other words, I needed to get really quiet, listen deeply, and then release something inside me for the circumstances to begin to shift.

In that light, the end of each chapter contains questions that can inspire you to see what you're still holding onto and where your Swiss cheese holes remain unfilled. You can answer them in a journal or even just muse on them in your head as you go about you day. The idea is to get things moving if they're stuck.

From my early childhood to that day in the cemetery, this book tells the story of the internal and external choices I've made throughout my life. It tells how my Swiss cheese holes were made and how I filled them up again. It describes how I have been able to live a limitless life in a powerless world by reaching within and consciously listening to my inner self, despite the challenges life has thrown my way. I hope that, by reading it, you can do the same.

Chapter 1

Setting the Foundation

For God has not given us a spirit of fear, but of
Power and of love and of a sound mind.

—2 Timothy 1:7 (NKJV)

Let's start at the beginning.

My parents set the foundation. As a little girl, I always felt we were living above the average standard for a middle-class family. We lived in Buffalo, New York, where both of my parents worked full-time jobs and then some. They showed my brother and me by example that hard work, dedication, and daily devotion to the family were what brought food to the table. Our bills were paid, and a world of happiness surrounded us. I felt limitless.

The mind power and man power of our family built our home. Our Polish heritage, which I'm very proud of, inspired us to pull together and realize my father's vision. Enduring countless hours of intense, hard labor, our whole family gathered during evenings and weekends to build our dream home, which I called the "White Castle."

My grandfather was at the center of our family. He had endless talents. Anything he wanted to know, he taught himself by trial and error. If something was more difficult, he signed himself up for a continuing-education class in his neighborhood. He continually showed my brother and me that with hard work, perseverance, and a lot of determination,

1

success was possible. I considered my grandfather to be the source of all my inspiration, drive, and creative imagination. There weren't any no's when I was a little girl; the answer was always, "Let's see what we can do," and then he brought us down to his basement workshop.

As a child, all his tools, nuts, bolts, pieces, and parts always intrigued me. There was an endless array of trinkets to create just about anything I could imagine. The place smelled like creation. My grandfather fixed everything in the neighborhood for everyone. If your lawn mower broke, you brought it over to Mr. Casey. If you wanted your hair trimmed or cut, or if you wanted a shave, he could do that too. Technically, he was a foreman at the local steel plant. But beyond that, he challenged his own mind each day, and by doing so, he challenged all of us.

My father took the challenge his father had set before him. A skilled cabinetmaker, he loves woodworking, building, and creating. He has a passion for life and lives simply. He dreamed he would build his own house for his family, so he did.

In 1973, when the city of Buffalo was beginning to change, many were thinking about moving to the "burbs," as they called it. This offered a life full of promise for raising young children outside the stifled city, away from the noisy buses and the congestion, and above all, away from the polluted air from the local factories. My parents set out and explored different lands slated for development. They wanted to own a special piece of property, one that would stay with our family for generations to come, a place where we could all grow up with a stable roof over our heads.

After many months of searching for a piece of property, they found the magical land. It was located in a rural area that felt hundreds of miles away from the city. At least it felt that way to me—it was far away from all I had known thus far in my young life. Most importantly, it was far away from my cousins, extended family, and my best friend, Carol Jean, who lived next door to my house in the city. There was a whole new world waiting there for us. It was something fresh, new, and undiscovered. I could feel my family's excitement in my bones. Although I was too young to understand the true impact the move would have on my life, my soul knew it was something pretty darn special. I felt special. I held my head higher, and I had a spring in my step.

My father's aunt gave him a personal loan to start the project. I am very grateful to that aunt, who is now deceased, for supporting my father's dream. In the end, he paid the loan back in full and never had to hold a mortgage. The property itself and the home he lovingly built on it left a legacy of fond memories. To this day, the White Castle continues to be a place where we can gather and reminisce about stories from the past.

My father gathered the family and explained his vision. Then he purchased the blueprints from an architect, and step by step, the hard work began. My brother and I visited on weekends to see the progress as my father, grandfather, uncles, and countless relatives worked day and night on our home for over a year. Watching this, I understood that anything in this world can be accomplished. Any thought, dream, or desire can be put into action and seen through.

Finally, one day, the white brick ranch house was finished.

I remember watching my grandfather plaster the last wall to perfection, secretly filling the walls with special energy. He was a man who lived with faith and inspired hope in every person he met. He was always smiling and joyful about life, happy to teach others and show them everything he knew. I learned many things from him in those early years: Don't ever give up. Persevere, and you will create the life you want. Find the joy and love in your heart, and you will be a magnet to others. Move away from negative energy and seek only the positive. Your garden will grow as you expand your mind and your thinking. Start with one simple plant; water, feed, and nurture it, and it will provide you with abundance in return.

I was seven years old when we moved in, and I felt like a princess. My brother and I ran through the hills, skipping and jumping over the mud puddles the rainstorm had left from the night before, surrounded by green grass and beautiful flowers. We were surrounded by wildlife, nature, and fields leading to the forest. The fresh air provided us with a sense of joy, hope, and new discovery. Many memories were to be made here over the years. Laughter and joy filled the walls of the house. Though, of course, we had heartaches, above all we were grateful and blessed. Our family's strong roots grew down through our house's very foundation.

I spent countless afternoons exploring the fields on foot with my doll and carriage in tow. Although we were only a thirty-minute drive from the city, it felt like we were a hundred miles away. To me, the place was paradise. The summer months brought bright sunshine that shone down on my face, and on endless warm summer nights, I lay in my bed, listening to the crickets sing in harmony. The sound provided me with calmness, a sense of being, and a promise for the new day that would follow. Life as we knew it was pretty simple.

The winters were quite harsh in upstate New York, and as I grew up, I was expected to pitch in and get us through. My father began a side business of selling firewood so he and my brother could earn extra money on the weekends. This meant spending many Saturday afternoons sitting on an upright wood round, helping them run the log splitter. I controlled the lever, running it back and forth as my father split loads of lumber. He and my brother delivered firewood to wealthy families in neighborhoods I only dreamed of living in. I sat for hours in the cold, bundled up in a snowsuit, hat, scarf, and gloves, most of the time with tears freezing to my rosy cheeks. All I wanted was to be in my warm house in front of the fireplace, writing poetry and creating imaginary tales about a little girl who got to run on the beach. As I sat by the log splitter, I couldn't wait to run back to the house for the hot chocolate and the hot homemade dinner my mother would have waiting for us. But in truth, we needed the money; the firewood sales paid for our extracurricular activities.

When we lived in the city, my mother had enrolled me in a weekly ballet class when I was five. It wasn't very successful; I have often listened to my mother tell the story of how I just stood there with my fingers in my mouth, crying. Now that I was seven years old, I begged my mother to enroll me in classes for tap and jazz.

My father was the breadwinner in our family. He was strict, and I feared him in some ways. At the same time, I felt my father's determination to show us how to earn a dollar, and teaching us lifelong skills were his way of showing love. When he forced our family to work together as a team, he was loving us.

Those long days of sitting in the bitter cold gave me the strength, courage, and determination to dream about what I did and didn't want for my life. I always felt there was something bigger, something powerful beyond anything I could ever even create. I just knew there was more to find, more to be, and a lot more to do.

When spring came, I made weekly trips with my mother to the city. Saturdays were my favorite; the early-morning drive from the countryside to the city always brought an exciting adventure. My mother, a hairdresser and aesthetician, needed to be ready with her pinking shears and straight-edge razor, because her first customer would be in the chair at nine a.m. sharp. While she tended to her elderly shampoo-and-set clientele, her desk filled up quickly with containers of homemade *chrusciki*, *pierogi*, and *placek*. All these baked goods and specially filled delicacies are traditional in Polish culture during the Easter season. My mother's clients were generous year-round; at Christmas, they brought a variety of homemade cookies. This was surely a perk of being a small-business owner. But Easter was my favorite. From Lent onward was simply delicious.

Although my mother is predominantly Italian, her father was Polish, and she inherited the great gene for cooking fabulous Polish dishes. She shared her love of baking with me, and this became a special time for us to bond. I remember standing on the step stool up against the kitchen counter while she taught me how to measure flour and sugar. I savored the smell of the vanilla extract while pouring a teaspoon into our favorite cookie recipe.

My mother's hair salon was directly across the street from the Roman Catholic Church in the dead center of a prominently Polish community. We have a deep-rooted, extended family throughout the area. My father grew up in the Polish part, and my mother grew up in the Italian neighborhood adjacent to it. Everyone knew everyone, and no one strayed far.

In such a tight-knit community, my parents let me be a "free-range" kid. As soon as I was able to check in all the morning clients, I could go off to meet my cousin Suzy. Suzy was a few years older than I, and our adventures gave us a great sense of freedom. I brought a few quarters for the bus ride and a few dollars for our window-shopping excursion, and we stayed downtown for the day.

I hopped and skipped all the way down the street a few blocks until I saw Suzy doing the same. We always met at our "halfway point," just a few blocks away from my mother's hair salon. First, we did our secret handshake, and then we spun around and embraced each other with a hug—always dressed as twins. One Saturday, it was purely accidental that we were wearing the same outfit, but it so delighted us that each Saturday thereafter we planned which matching outfits to wear the following week. We either tried to coordinate our colors with matching hair ribbons or had our parents purchase the same outfits for us.

Neither of us had a sister, and we both had one brother. Together, we were inseparable twins.

We walked to the bus stop to wait for our usual 11:20 a.m. Saturday morning 20B route, which would take us to the small downtown shopping district. The trip was the highlight of the week. We boarded the bus together and sat in the same seats every week, giggling and laughing about the stories of the week from our respective schools.

Suzy and I were very mature for our age. We loved having our matching leather banana-shaped purses over our shoulders. They came in all colors of leather—from bright yellow to subtle colors like black, caramel, and wine. We felt as if we were eighteen years old.

Once we arrived downtown, our first stop was always Fanny Farmer for chocolate candy cigarettes wrapped in colored foil and packaged in a plastic container. And then we wandered over to Hickory Farms cheese and d'oeuvres shop to collect all the free samples we could. Sometimes the woman who worked there gave us extras. Next we were off to lunch at our favorite, Burger King. The best part about this Burger King was that it was a two-story building. We loved to sit up near the second-floor window seat overlooking Main Street and the shopping district, thinking we were so cool. We beamed with pride because we were trusted to do all this without adults.

I could never have dreamed that I'd be treated more like an independent adult at ten years old than I would later in life. Little did I know that the feeling of being limitless would be nonexistent as a thirty-year-old married woman with two children.

Though my parents made me work hard for what I wanted, they weren't controlling. I learned that love and trust went hand in hand. My mother showed me how women could work hard, my father inspired me to live my dreams, and my grandfather taught me to do so with creativity, perseverance, and kindness. It was a limitless childhood; life as I knew it was footloose and fancy free.

Questions for Reflection

1. Who has inspired you in your life?
2. What lessons did you learn from this person?
3. What settings or situations inspire you?

Chapter 2

Independence

Never regret anything because at one time
it was exactly what you wanted.

—Marilyn Monroe

By the time I turned seventeen, my daily schedule was full of tap, jazz, and ballet classes. When school got out at the end of the day, I drove to my local dance school, where I spent many hours practicing, teaching, and performing. It was 1986, near the end of the school year, and I was determined to earn more money to reach my savings goal by the end of the summer. I dreamed of traveling abroad to Europe. Teaching dance wasn't going to bring in enough, and as I began to look for another job that summer, my dance teacher suggested I try the local dance shop and set up an appointment for me. On Pointe Dance Shop was where we purchased our dance shoes, leotards, tights, and anything else we needed to put on a show. With my passion for dance, my knowledge of the products, and the retail experience I had gained through working my first job a few years before, I felt this would be a great fit. With great excitement, I prepared to drive into the city for my interview.

Little did I know that stepping into this charming shop would change my life forever. It was an old building, built in the early 1900s. The old wood floor creaked when I stepped into the shop, and the smell of leather dance shoes filled the air. Hundreds upon hundreds of white and black shoeboxes filled the shelves. I was told to ask for a man named Mr. M.

As I entered, the bells on the door brought a short, young, dark-haired gentleman out from the back storeroom. "May I help you?" he asked.

"Um, yes, I am here to see Mr. M. I am here for a job interview."

"He is out on an errand right now," the gentleman replied. I must have had a perplexed look on my face since we'd made an appointment. "Oh, it's okay. My name is Rick, and I can help you. One moment please."

Rick walked to the back of the store and came back with a pen and a yellow legal pad held by a clipboard. "Please have a seat," he said with a warm smile.

I first noticed that Rick had big, deep, dark-brown eyes with a bit of a twinkle. Then I noticed his warm and comforting smile. Although I felt a bit intimidated by him, I listened intently to the questions he asked me. He asked me about my dance history and my prior retail experience, jotting down notes on his yellow legal pad as I answered. But mostly he stared at me as if his eyes were looking deep into my soul. It wasn't an uncomfortable feeling; it was as if I were meant to be there. My soul had found its home in that moment. He continued on with a few more questions and then said, "Well, when can you start?"

"Start?" I replied in a state of confusion. "Start what?"

"You came here for a job, right?"

I nodded.

"Okay, when can you start? We can employ you as soon as possible."

I smiled. I was so excited that I felt compelled to say, *Tomorrow!* Instead, I paused and said, "I can start on Monday. What time should I be here?"

I walked out of On Pointe, feeling like I was on top of the world. What could be better than being surrounded with hundreds of ballet shoes, pointe shoes, tap shoes, and all the glitz and glam every day?

I crossed the street with a spring in my step, walking to my car with thoughts of financial freedom. After all, at seventeen years of age, all I wanted was to be independent from my parents and show them I was well on my way to taking care of myself. Plus, I had a goal: I would save my own money and go on an awesome adventure in Europe. It was quickly approaching the fall of 1986. I knew the work lined up for me would take my heart to greater distances. The summer abroad in 1987 would enrich my life trifold.

The adventure I had begun to plan and map out in my mind was taking shape. I felt I was now making decisions for myself based on what was right for me. And given my small-town background, it wasn't a common choice; escaping from the everyday normalcy of life to travel abroad was something no one in my family had ever done. The thought of coming back and having new insight and a broader perspective of the world increased my excitement. It would be fantastic for my résumé. Broadening my horizons and expanding my awareness through travel held a perfect place for future career potential.

I was excited about the job, but I had no idea that that day would forever change my world. I had just been interviewed by the man who would become my boss, my husband, and the father of our children in years to come. I am fortunate that our souls met. We ended up sharing half a lifetime together, and we were bountifully blessed with three incredible, strong, courageous children. But at seventeen, I had no way of even imagining such a thing.

By the time I started work the following Monday, I had come to realize that Rick was the son of the owner, Mr. M. They worked together side by side seven days a week. They were both strong-willed with brilliant minds, and they stuck together like glue.

The store had several locations. In the early years, I began working at their original location with Rick. He taught me a great deal, leading by example as I followed behind. I watched and listened intently. I was a fast learner. And I quickly picked up that he had quite a reputation in the world of ballerinas—especially those who wore the hard-toed, satin pointe shoes. Rick had an incredible eye and a real talent for assessing ballerinas' feet. His eyes took in the size, shape, and width of every pair of feet that walked through the front door. His customers would drive great distances to meet the man known as the expert pointe shoe fitter of Western New York.

Before a customer even sat down in the fitting chair, he already had the shoe that would best fit the shape of her foot in his hand. On Pointe stocked an expansive selection of shoes from all over the world—ballet shoes handcrafted in London, Brazil, and the USA; and the famous Sansha pointe shoes handcrafted in China. Rick—or Mr. Rick, as his customers called him—kept inventory of a variety of sizes and widths to fit almost any foot. His incredible reputation and consistent customer base grew over the years by word of mouth, mostly due to the great pride he took with his shoe fittings. Mr. Rick always went the extra mile to put a smile on each dancer's face. His job satisfaction came when he could solve the most complex problem for a dancer or dance teacher. If a ballerina needed extra strength to her shoe, he figured how to add it. If another ballerina were constantly slipping, he glued rubber on the base of her shoe. He was always thinking about how to better serve his customers, and his patience with them was exceptional.

Fitting a pointe shoe properly is a specialized skill, and after many years, I began to pick it up. I learned to recite the way he spoke, the vocabulary he used with each customer. Spending hours upon hours working together for so many years, we learned a lot about each other, too. I felt proud working next to Rick. He was powerful, and he made me feel powerful. He had gained a lot of integrity over the years by working at his family business.

In fact, I worked with the whole family. A tight-knit unit of Italians, they worked the business together. Rick's lovely mother went by the name of Mrs. M. She ran the suburban location closest to the family home. Mr. M., of course, ran the main location. Then there were siblings and aunts and uncles and cousins. As a young girl, I was pretty enamored with their family. Even when I was working with a bunch of hotheaded Italians, there was something that drew me in. They welcomed me like a member of the family. It was important for me to have a good work ethic. Their booming small business was nothing like my prior retail experience at a large corporate department store. I loved being embraced by a large, loud Italian family.

Was it the love they all had for each other in the midst of their craziness that drew me in? It could get pretty wild during the long working days, but regardless of what happened, once the shop closed, they always went home together to gather over pasta and several glasses of red wine. Weekends were full of events, too; when I returned to work on Monday, Rick's family often talked about the great meals they had shared together. They spent many long hours cooking a special spaghetti sauce every Sunday. I was intrigued and eager to learn about this secret recipe, which they shared only with family members.

In truth, I envied the closeness their family shared. Most nights after work, I just drove back home and retreated to my childhood room. My house felt quiet in comparison. I never shared a glass of wine with my parents—or any sort of drink with them, for that matter. My father didn't have much to say in the evening. He was tired from working several jobs. My mother had a long commute home after working a full day at her hair salon in the city, only ever leaving work early if she had a Mary Kay meeting or a special event to attend.

I admired my parents; they worked hard for our family. At the same time, I longed for the days of my childhood when our large extended family drove out to our beautiful house to spend lazy Sunday afternoons. My grandparents came every Sunday, and a couple of times a month, the whole family came to gather. My mother prepared summer salads while my father lit charcoal briquettes on the grill. I cherished those special days, which had diminished by the time I went to work at On Pointe.

In part, this was because my family was going through a painful time with my grandfather's health. He was dying from cancer. At seventeen, I was pretty much kept in the dark about this; I wasn't able to grasp the serious nature of his illness, and I didn't fully understand he was preparing to transition away until it was imminent. My mind was full of the exciting, new job I had taken on that summer. I daydreamed about my grand expectations for the life I was building. No one close to me had ever died, and somehow I just didn't see the end coming until it came.

My grandfather was my everything. He was very much a father figure to me. He was my mentor, my provider; he was the person I went to for advice. Later in life, I learned that my parents were trying to spare me from the pain of seeing him so sick and losing him, but this shielding me left me unprepared for the loss.

Just a few days before Thanksgiving, he went home to be with the

Lord. Our Thanksgiving dinner that year was quiet and full of grief. The women in our family surrounded our dining table, writing thank-you cards to everyone who had attended his wake and funeral. I escaped to the solitude of my bedroom and hid from the pain and agony that adorned everyone's face. My father didn't speak. My mother scurried around the kitchen, trying to keep herself busy. Shocked by his death, I grieved in private.

Soon thereafter, I stopped going to church. I didn't understand why the person I loved so much, the one I had cherished and had the utmost respect for, the man who had taught me everything about life, could be taken from me when I was at such a critical age. I was furious with grief.

I came across a groundbreaking book on grief by Elizabeth Kubler-Ross. Her words inspired me and gave me hope again. Slowly, I came to see that while my grandfather might have been visually gone, he still walked alongside me. When I stopped being mad and let God back into my life, many things started to change for the better. My attitude had changed completely as I began to understand these hard life lessons. At night I prayed on my knees next to my bed, just like you see in children's picture books. I asked to feel my grandfather near me and for him to help me in my life. I asked for him to continue to guide and help me make decisions. I asked for God to help me, too.

Returning to prayer lifted my spirits, and good things started to happen to me. I received a $1,000 check from the Polish Federation, money my grandfather had saved for me. The check propelled me to work harder and save more money. The gift was like winning the lottery, and I knew that with just a little more saving, I would be ready to take my trip.

Back in 1986 and 1987, it seemed like everyone was going to Europe to backpack, travel, and explore. I thought this sounded like an incredible opportunity. We didn't have any computers or Internet to get information; there weren't any websites, forums, or blogs to read up on what to do or where to go. Most people went to their local travel agency to collect brochures, book tickets, and get information.

I'd always been a big reader, so I went to our local public library. I read books on England, France, Italy, and Greece. All the places fascinated me; I just couldn't stop reading. I continued my search by going to our local travel agency. Sitting down with the agent, I told her my plan. She handed me many brochures to take home. At the weekly Mary Kay meetings I attended with my mother, I learned how to use a vision board to attain a goal or dream. After the long days at On Pointe, I sat in my childhood bedroom, carefully cutting photos out of the brochures and gluing them to my vision board.

Zeroing in on my plans for Europe was the first step toward healing my inner self after losing my grandfather. My focus had shifted. I was no longer focused on my loss but instead on what I could make out of it. This was important; I just knew it. I reminded myself that my grandfather would have wanted me to see as much of the world as possible. I felt him all throughout my planning process while I worked hard to earn the funds to go.

I also decided I didn't want to go alone, so I contacted my childhood friend Karena. She was a very hard worker and held several jobs. She agreed to join my adventure, and the plan was set.

I finally earned enough money to put down a deposit on the Eurorail pass, which I quickly discovered was the best and most economical way to travel in and out of different countries throughout Europe. Following the travel agent's advice, I purchased the airline tickets well ahead of time to get the best price. Then I bought a copy of the *Frommer's Guide* and began looking at youth hostels. On July 11, 1987, Karena and I took a limo taxi to the Toronto airport and embarked on one of the most incredible journeys either of us would ever experience.

Along the way, we both discovered that a lot of lessons are learned; though challenges rose and obstacles appeared in front of us, we kept right on going. I kept to the spiritual practice I'd developed in the wake of my grandfather's death, praying in every city and paying my respects in every chapel, cathedral, and duomo I could find. I witnessed many magical experiences, and I knew the impossible couldn't have happened without the help of spirit—an angel, guide, or God looking down on me. Though I was still quite young and a bit naïve, I felt the presence of my grandfather more than ever. I believe he supported my journey far beyond the $1,000 check, guiding and protecting me all along the way.

In the end, what I experienced was beyond anything I could have ever imagined. The trip abroad was truly a life-changing experience for me, one I carry with me throughout my adult travels with gratitude and love in my heart.

Questions for Reflection

1. Have you ever felt entirely independent?
2. How did that experience affect you?
3. What could you do right now to bring that same effect into your life?

Chapter 3

A Limitless Journey

*E*verything you have collected throughout your life—all the places you have visited, the experiences, traumas, and tragedies that have endured—are strands that weave together to make up the threads of your soul. As you travel throughout life, you continue to add to your threads until you have enough to weave into a blanket. This is the blanket you wrap around your heart.

Europe had endless sunsets. Karena and I took midnight strolls along the warm waters of the Aegean Sea, looking over spectacular views of the buildings, whitewashed and topped with a splash of blue. The eight weeks were entirely carefree. I explored the Parisian streets, pausing to sip a café au lait accompanied by a *pain au chocolat* while enjoying the most magical, sparkly view of the Tour de Eiffel. This particular memory—sitting alone at an outdoor café on the streets of Paris—became a reoccurring, vivid dream for me. The option to choose from the varied selection of pastries reminded me of my early childhood adventures with my cousin. There seemed to be a pattern of excitement growing within me. Anytime I was able to make my own choices without an adult hovering over my shoulders was enlightening.

I got a taste of the European lifestyle—one my palate never forgot. The memories were embedded in my mind and cherished in my heart. Later, I embraced any opportunity I had to talk about the eight-week holiday, which broadly changed my view about myself, society, and what I learned from the most spectacular cities in the world. With each conversation I felt my soul light up like a Christmas tree. I relished the opportunity to reminisce on the great and independent adventure I had taken in my late teenage years.

It started with Karena and me saying goodbye to our families and loading our heavy, overstuffed backpacks into our limo. Since we had purchased the lowest-priced airline tickets out of Toronto, Canada, our travel agency arranged the two-hour drive for us from Buffalo.

Things were different then. We traveled without a cell phone or the Internet. There weren't any couch-surfing sites to log into. It was strictly the *Frommer's Guide*. We held onto that book like it was our bible. Embedded within the pages were the names of the contacts we made on the train, the promises we made (and kept) to meet up in three days or two weeks, and our meeting time and place. Remarkably, we found that the friends we'd made kept their promises, too; there they were, standing on the corner and leaning up against the lamppost, backpack and all, grinning from ear to ear as they waited for us. We made connections and kept them, trusting our new friends in a way that is nearly obsolete today. All the handwritten notes, names and addresses, train ticket stubs, and hotel receipts are still in my journal from thirty-one years ago.

Those pages are stained with early-morning coffee spills, dust, dirt, and grease, bringing me to reminisce on a time I could never forget. It is the independence I felt that keeps those memories alive. When I look back, I think far less about the great adventure—the sights and sounds of the Parisian streets or the honking of the red London buses or black taxis. What comes to the forefront is the independence my life held in that time period. At nineteen years old, the trip to Europe was one of my life's biggest accomplishments: a journey I successfully completed on my own and one I was damn proud of. I was able to execute my plan through intent, purpose, and action. To this day, it is something no one can strip from me. It is mine.

Looking back, we were just two naïve girls about to take a trip of a lifetime. We were both very responsible but had no idea what we were about to endure. I felt I had done my homework and had everything mapped out perfectly, right down to the number of days we would spend in each city and the costs of lodging and food. Our Eurorail ticket was already prepaid. This wise purchase would help us get through the countries we anxiously wanted to visit.

But right from the beginning I had to learn that the trip would take its own course; Mother Nature had something else in mind. A huge summer thunderstorm came through Toronto. We had already boarded the aircraft and were buckled in our seats. We sat on the runway for quite some time before the pilot's voice came over the loudspeaker. The flight was canceled due to the thunder and lightning storms in the area and wouldn't be leaving until the following morning. There were moans and groans from the passengers. As it turned out, if it hadn't been for that overnight flight delay, we would have never met three incredible friends, who later would play a very important role in our journey.

The airline offered us vouchers for a hotel nearby the airport. We stood in line to receive them, giggling and gleaming with delight about our journey ahead. The delayed flight couldn't even damper our excitement. It became a huge part of our adventure. The colored threads were already beginning to slowly weave together.

Three Greek men stood behind us in line. As we discussed the flight delay, we met them: Stavros, Christophe, and Costa. Together we rode the bus to the nearby airport hotel. Karena and I immediately connected with our new Greek friends. We all sat together to eat with our food vouchers. As we got acquainted and shared our proposed itinerary with them, it was enlightening to find how impressed they were with us.

Our conversation quickly led to our plans for Greece and our visiting the islands. Greece had been on our list, but we weren't quite certain whether we had enough time to get there. After an extensive conversation about the incredible landscape and the clear, tranquil waters, Karena and I both simply knew the Greek islands had risen to the top of our list.

The next morning we headed to the Toronto airport to board our flight to London. After getting settled in our seats, we realized we were just a few rows away from our Greek friends. It was comforting to know we had our travel companions with us.

We planned to spend just two days in London at the beginning of our trip before flying to Dublin, Ireland. My college roommate, Marguerite, was from the outskirts of Dublin, in County Kildare. Marguerite had come to the USA to study for two years, and we had been in several classes together. I was really quite fond of her—in fact, our friendship was a big part of my planning this trip abroad. She would be our first stop and a comforting one.

Karena and I were greatly looking forward to staying at a nearby bed-and-breakfast in County Kildare. It sounded so homelike, and after traveling for four days, it was a rest we needed complete with a traditional Irish plate of bacon, sausages, puddings, eggs, vegetables, and potatoes. The meal was served with a generous helping of homemade Irish soda bread and a strong cup of breakfast tea.

Marguerite picked us up from the airport in a very small car. We weren't quite sure whether our large, heavy backpacks would fit. She lifted up the boot and smashed them down, and off we went. We were wedged into her little, red Dacia Sandero like sardines in a tuna can as Marguerite sped off into the countryside. We passed through valleys and pastures of the brightest green before arriving in County Kildare. It was wonderful to catch up with my college friend and meet the family she had spoken of so fondly—truly an honor.

The Irish countryside was a picturesque sight, just like I'd seen in the movies. There were rolling green pastures filled with farm animals, and each bit of rain brought the rainbows I had imagined. My heart filled with joy. and I found myself taking in a slower-paced culture that made me reminisce a bit about my childhood in the countryside. This place had a similar feel, but it was much more charming. The Irish dialect fascinated me.

My friend Marguerite planned to take us out to a traditional Irish pub, complete with a dance of the Irish jig. The air was filled with the smell of Irish brew. Seeing a pint of beer being passed along to her friends seated at our table was another first for me. Cheers and rowdy Irish men filled our small space. Karena and I were definitely getting a true Irish blessing.

A few short days later, we moved on. We had planned on taking the boat from the dock in Ireland to Le Havre France. From Le Havre we could take the train, using our Eurorail pass to get to Paris. As it turned out, it wasn't a pleasant boat trip. I wasn't quite prepared for the excessive heavy waves of the Atlantic, especially since our tickets put us in the bottom quarters for nearly twenty-one hours. It was one of the longest nights of my life.

After a two-hour train ride, recovering from the nausea left behind from the boat trip, our fragile bodies couldn't wait to get checked into the youth hostel we had prebooked. Our high expectations of getting to one of the most magical cities in Europe gave me the strength I needed to put one foot in front of the other. The long walk off the train platform over to the taxi stand while loaded down with an overstuffed aluminum-framed backpack nearly made me fall over. What was I thinking?

Landing in our first big foreign city, being unable to speak the French language, and having to navigate our way from the train station to our destination were a bit tricky, to say the least. Karena and I quickly realized this journey wasn't going to be so easy. It was getting harder as the days passed by. We had now been traveling for a little over a week.

After we arrived and got settled at our youth hostel, located in the 15th arrondissement, I lay my tired body down between the crisp, hard linen sheets. They smelled like the dry cleaners. There was nothing at all comforting here in this stark room. It reminded me of a hospital. I swung open the rusted window, hoping to get some air flowing through the stuffy room. It was a hot, still night.

Tears began to flow down my face. Homesickness hit me in Paris, France, of all places. Here I was, in the city of lights, a magical place filled with history, architecture, and culture; and I was miserable. In retrospect, I think I just needed to close my eyes and get a good night's sleep.

But that was hard to come by. Within a few hours. we awoke to very loud, drunken travelers trying to get settled in the vacant room next to us. I had fallen asleep with tears of exhaustion flowing down my face, so when I woke up, there were still strands of light-blonde hair dried to my cheek. I lay on the hard mattress, listening to the drunken travelers fall against our adjoining wall. I prayed they would soon settle in while I watched the white linen eyelet curtains, hanging in the old rusted windows, sway in the moonlit sky. "Welcome to Paris," I softly whispered to myself.

When morning came, our stark. white room was filled with bright sunlight. It was time to get up and find the magic in this city I had dreamed about for years. Somehow my inner self was screaming that the task wouldn't be so simple.

I was in desperate need to get near some water. I hoped a long walk along the Pont Mirabeau, staring out over the River Seine with a magnificent view of the Eiffel Tower, would soften my homesick heart. I darted out quickly while Karena was still asleep. My plan worked. Stepping out of our youth hostel and taking a walk along the cobblestone streets to find this incredible bridge helped clear my fuzzy head. Passing by an array of cafés and watching all the onlookers made me want to stop, sit, and capture the beauty, so I did just that.

Once I sat down, things again became more complicated. I found the menu to be very challenging, and trying to get the waiter's attention to order a cafe au lait wasn't simple. I sat and wondered what the trick was to get the waiter to stop at my table and take my order as I watched him pass by again and again. Not wanting to feel frustrated, I tried to wave him down again. He whizzed by me again. *Huh*, I thought. *Maybe if I smile, he will stop.* He whizzed by me again. Then I remembered something my *Frommer's Guide* had indicated in the section on navigating the streets of Paris. I closed my menu to signal to the waiter that I was ready to order. It worked! He immediately halted. "*Bonjour, madame,*" he said. "*Que voulez vous commander?*"

I answered that I wanted to order one cafe au lait and then proceeded to point to a *pain au chocolat*. He delivered my order, and it was perfect.

After my walk and my solo breakfast, I returned to the hostel. Karena and I spent the afternoon visiting the Jardin de Luxembourg, a gorgeous park that included a lot of ground to cover. We enjoyed some quiet time, playing with the small, colorful sailboats in the water. The tradition is to push them with a stick, and we joined in. It was relaxing and fun to hear the gleeful sounds of the small French children.

We didn't stay very long in the magical city of lights. It was really expensive, and Karena and I both desperately needed the seaside. However, the visit was just enough for my soul to get a taste of Parisian life, creating a memory that would forever be embedded within.

After a few days in Paris, we packed up and headed to the train station in the 10th arrondissement. Traveling by train during the night hours meant we could grab a sleeper car, which saved us from having to purchase a room in the youth hostel or at an expensive hotel. We took the night train down to the south of France to see the Cote d' Azur, visiting Monte Carlo, Nice, and Monaco. We were excited to finally reach some warmer weather. We threw our backpacks onto the heavily rocked, pebbled beaches, welcoming the sunshine and cooler blue waters of the Mediterranean, which revived our fatigued and weary selves.

Our travel itinerary then brought us to Zurich, Switzerland. The city of Zurich was a place I had always wanted to visit. As a bonus, like in Ireland, in Zurich we had friends to see.

About a year before, on a gray day in Niagara Falls, New York, Karena and I had met three kind gentlemen from Zurich. We had purchased tickets to board "The Maid of Mist," a boat tour that would take us underneath Niagara Falls. Three very tall men were in line ahead of us. My barely five-foot-two self couldn't see around them. Coming from a family of short stature, I had never been in the company of men that tall. My ear quickly picked up on their Swiss-German language, and I was immediately intrigued. Inching my way closer and trying to make myself noticed, I was eager to strike up a conversation with one or all of them. Of course, my gorgeous friend Karena, with her tall model figure, blue-green eyes, and dark-brown hair, instantly caught the eye of one of the gentlemen. The line began to move, and we started to talk as the first rain drops fell. By the time we boarded the boat, yellow plastic rain ponchos were passed out to each guest. There we were, all primped and looking tan in our best summer fashion, and we had to put a yellow plastic rain poncho on over our cute outfits to go underneath the mist of Niagara Falls. Beyond that, our hair was puffy in the style of 1986. Between the mist and the now-pouring rain, we both ended up looking like dead rats. Who were we trying to impress?

Little did we know that these European men weren't at all interested in our hair; they were just excited to be speaking with two American teenage girls. The whole experience felt liberating; I, too, wanted to know more about them. This was my first exposure to a different culture.

We ended up having a wonderful dinner and exchanging addresses and phones numbers, and we soon realized we had met and made an incredible friendship.

One late summer morning in 1986, I opened my mailbox, and there was a colorful envelope. The international postage was a clear indicator that it had come from Switzerland. My heart raced with anticipation. I quickly ran up our stone driveway and into the house, racing down the long hallway to my bedroom. I jumped up onto my twin bed and read the words of my new Swiss friend, whom I had met only a few weeks before. I carefully ripped open the envelope with a butter knife, wanting to keep it all beautiful and intact. The bright-orange envelope was filled with a heavier-weighted egg-blue-colored stationery. I had never seen anything like it. I carefully read every word.

This was my first experience in corresponding with a European man. He spoke Swiss German and English, and his English was very good. Erich and I continued to write for a whole year. He told me that, if we ever visited Europe, we should be sure to travel to Switzerland; I would love the country. Sure enough, as I planned my trip, I wrote Switzerland down on my list of favorite places to visit. I dreamed every night about what it would be like to experience something so unimaginable and far away.

Like my plans to visit Marguerite, I could hardly believe it when my dream became a reality. A year later, I found myself checking into a five-star Zurich hotel, complete with fluffy down comforters and down pillows. The next day we called our friends. They met us, and the long weekend adventure began.

Europeans live and work to play. They work hard, but they also take the time for peaceful, restful relaxation. This was immediately evident when we arrived at the river to find kayaks waiting for us. Our Swiss friends came very prepared with all the equipment we would need for our adventurous afternoon, including a life vest for each of us and a picnic lunch. Lying back and relaxing in the kayak while floating down the river in Zurich filled my heart with joy. I felt there was a whole world of possibilities waiting for me. I felt limitless.

Karena and I were both in awe that these men, who barely knew us, would show us such amazing hospitality. It was an event I had never experienced back in the USA with anyone my age. I was so taken. Karena and I had a wonderful weekend with our Swiss friends. Everything about our visit to Switzerland was perfect. Our trip visiting our friends had gone off without a hitch, and Switzerland itself had truly captured my heart. But once again, it was time for us to move on with our itinerary.

After Zurich, Karena and I took the train down to Italy, stopping in Milan, Florence, and Venice. By this point we were eager to get to Greece. We took our final Italian train from Venice to Brindisi, where there is a large port housing boats, ships, and ferries. This is where we would board the ferry to cross the Ionian Sea and dock in Athens.

Except for a short hiccup between Ireland and Paris, our plans had gone off without a hitch. Everything had been perfect, and we were limitless. I had no idea I was about to face one of the most powerless moments of my life.

Questions for Reflection

1. When have you ever stepped out of your comfort zone?
2. What do you desire for yourself?
3. To what extent are you willing to step out of your comfort zone to attain those desires?

Chapter 4

Powerless in Greece

Not until we are lost do we begin to understand ourselves.

—Henry David Thoreau

The planes, trains, and automobiles made it a truly remarkable journey. My hair and clothing were filled with the smell of diesel fuel pumping from the funnel of the Grecian ferry liner. An eight-hour ferry ride from Athens to the island of Mykonos and then a quick hop over to Ios left a journal full of love, names, addresses, and phones numbers. I felt fairly confident and good about myself at this point; Karena and I had just one week left before we would take the boat back off the island to the mainland. We thought it would be smooth sailing. Little did we know our friendship was about to be put to the test.

Our plane tickets would take us from Athens back to London after the time we spent on the islands. The plan was to capture the last few days of independence while exploring Oxford Street, Regent, and Bond. I imagined us stepping up on a red double-decker and whirling around Piccadilly to land on Brompton Road and drink tea at Harrods.

But first we were slated to meet up with Stavros, Christophe, and Costa in Athens. We were full of excitement as we boarded the ferry in Brindisi, Italy. We found a phone booth soon after we disembarked from the ferry and rang them. They gave us directions to meet them.

Connecting with our friends from our very first flight to Toronto was wonderful. After a night in Athens, we began our travels onward to the islands. Like we'd experienced in Ireland and Switzerland, it was wonderful to have local friends as our guides. As we navigated the most magical places my eyes had ever seen, I could finally relax and let my guard down a bit since I no longer had to figure out where to go or what to do. Upon arriving on the island of Ios, our friends directed us to a youth hostel, where a classic Greek grandmotherly type known as Yia-Yia housed travelers. She looked after her guests and kept their passports and possessions safe while they sunbathed on the pebble sand beaches. Our backpacks had become heavier with each step on the cobblestone streets, made up of winding narrow pathways that twisted and turned around rows of whitewashed buildings. As we passed numerous charming, quaint artisan shops and cafés, I took in the scenery—but had no idea where we were going. I was just happy that someone else was leading the way.

We came upon a house that looked more or less like the rest though surrounded by beautiful flowers. Our friends introduced us to Yia-Yia, and she showed us our sleeping quarters. She was truly a kind woman. I appreciated her spirit and the clean beds tightly made up with crisp, white linens. As tired as I was, I didn't want to stay; my spirit was hungry for the Aegean Sea. I was greatly looking forward to resting my withered self on Manganari Beach. The allure of the clean, clear waters bought solace to my being. Karena and I quickly left for the water, rolling our woven mats out over the wide, pebbled stone shore. Rows of dark-skinned, tan bodies were lined to soak up the hot sun. In 1987, Greece was in the middle of a heat wave. It was one of the hottest summers in history, reaching scalding temperatures of over 100 degrees Fahrenheit.

Ios had a reputation for being the best party island. Many young travelers rested and sunbathed by day and partied by night. Personally, I wasn't big on the night scene. I had barely experimented with alcohol, which was still illegal for me in my home country since I was just nineteen. But beyond our Greek friends, we met new travelers from Germany, Italy, and Bermuda; and they all wanted to celebrate the end of summer. With just four days left before departing back to London, we decided we would join the party.

Back at Yia-Yia's that evening, Karena and I washed the hot sand from our sunburned bodies. Even though we had applied sunscreen, we were red and blistered; we couldn't even think about laying the cotton towels Yia-Yia had left for us on our skin. After showering, we quickly scampered up the back stone staircase and onto the rooftop, where we bared our blistered, naked bodies, hoping to catch a cool night wind. We took turns pouring pure aloe on our burnished skin, allowing it to dry in the breeze.

Yia-Yia collected everyone's passport for safekeeping. It seemed like overkill, but I certainly respected her old school values. The twinkle in her eye and her dried, wrinkled face told me a story. I knew she had been through a lifetime of evenings on the island of Ios; she just wanted to keep us safe.

Donning the lightest cotton dresses we could find, off we went. We followed our new friends through more winding cobblestone streets to the center of Ios's nightlife. We stopped at a beach club bar near the water and found ourselves surrounded by tan bodies, each polished and primped for an evening of drinks and conversation. Gentle breezes blew our sun-kissed hair, while the rhythmic sounds of music had our bodies swaying to the beat.

I told myself I was merely going out for the social aspect and to people-watch. I wasn't a drinker, nor a big partier, but I really enjoyed listening to music, engaging in conversation, and mingling with a crowd. Our friends purchased rounds of ouzo, a Greek anise flavored liquer, and passed them to us. Karena and I mingled through the thick crowd, drinks in hand, taking turns talking to travelers and natives. It was exciting to meet different people and learn where they were from, seeing such a wide variety of ethnic backgrounds, religions, and beliefs about life.

As the night progressed with more dancing, drinks, and loud music, I lost track of Karena. She often went off on her own, so I didn't think much of it. Soon it was well into the early morning hours, and the bar was still hopping with people. I found myself talking to new friends, who introduced me to new friends and new friends after that. Eventually, I ended up hanging out with a guy from Toronto. As the conversation progressed, I realized I'd lost track of Stavros, Christophe, and Costa, too.

A group of us, including my new friend from Toronto, decided to get away from the crowd and take a walk along the beach. Since there were a lot of people down by the water, I figured I would find Karena there, too. The air was much cooler. My body was exhausted from a day in the sun and my first taste of ouzo. At some point, I realized I really wanted to go sleep at Yia-Yia's, but I didn't know the way back on my own. I hoped to find my girlfriend and our Greek friends so someone could show me the way.

Chatting and strolling along, we settled down into the sand. The moonlit sky shone so brightly; I was sure someone I knew would pass by soon. I lay back and watched as the night sky reflected off the ripples of the sea, the crisp, clear water swallowed beneath the pebbled shore.

I remember being very tired, even more than usual. But amid the sun, the long day, and the ouzo …

I woke up to the sunrise, pebbles stuck to my face. Waves crashed against the shore and the rocks. Where was I?

Holy shit, I thought. I took a look around; there were only a few stragglers spread along the beach, all passed out from the party the night before. Where was the guy I had met from Toronto? Was I dreaming? Had he even been real? Where were my friends?

I sat up and fumbled around, looking for my purse. At first, I didn't want to think that my purse was snatched. I knew I'd had the purse when we left the bar, and I knew I'd had it here with me on the beach. I'd used it under my head as a pillow. Everything I needed to get back to the mainland was in there. Our ferry tickets. The rest of my money. The only thing that thankfully wasn't in my purse was my passport—small consolation, given the circumstances. I searched the sand, looking for my purse in the radius around me. There were only the glistening pebbles of sand.

My purse was gone.

How can I get back to Yia-Yia's? I was in a full panic; I needed to find my way back. As I stood up, I searched for my mental compass. Every nerve in my body had become loose as I tried to remember, tried to make sense of what had just happened during the night. What man would leave a woman alone here on the beach? I didn't know whether the guy from Toronto had taken my purse or whether a stranger walking the beach had taken it from beneath me while I was asleep. The thought of either option was terrifying.

I ran off, breathing heavily and not even knowing which direction I was headed. I got up the sand hill and sat down on a stone wall. The tears welled up in my eyes and poured down my face. I thought of my grandfather, whose thousand-dollar check had helped send me to Europe. I thought of my family, who had trusted me to take this adventure. My mind whirled with painful questions.

Who took my purse? How did I let myself drink and become so vulnerable? But more than that: *How could my best friend just leave me like this? Where is she? Is she okay?*

I wondered whether she had gone off with our Greek friends and was back at Yia-Yia's, safely sleeping. *She must have; she must be,* I told myself.

I sat. I prayed. I prayed to my grandfather and anyone who would listen.

Luckily, I had grown up with a good sense of direction. My independence required me to take responsibility for myself at a young age. My parents didn't coddle me; they expected that I took responsibility for my whereabouts from early on. I thought of my ten-year-old self riding the bus downtown. *I must be able to find my way,* I emphatically said to myself.

I pulled myself together and tried to think of a plan. Perhaps I could just start walking, and then I could ask some locals along the way. Surely someone would recognize my description of the wonderful old woman who cared for so many year after year.

But it was still too early. The sun was barely up—the white stone streets were bare. Empty. An eerie silence prevailed. I walked through the town. Up steps, down steps. I turned right, then left. Then straight up. I followed something I had never known before. It was as if my body had gone into survival mode, or perhaps there was a divine being pushing me along the way. As I walked, my mind ran quickly, sweeping through the filmlike quality of the night before. Everything on an island in Greece looks the same. But I did manage to notice a few landmarks from when we'd come down the hill last night. Some things looked familiar. Not enough things but some.

After some time, the tears began to stream down my face again. I choked on my dry mouth. My eyes swept over signs along the way.

Restaurant and café signs. Hostels, lodging signs. I couldn't be sure that I truly recognized any of them.

I longed to see Yia-Yia's bright and beautiful flowers. I kept telling myself, *I am sorry. I am sorry.* I took great fault in the situation; I felt guilty about the ouzo and felt that I should have been more responsible. *How could I have let myself get so out of control?*

I promised myself and my grandfather that if I could just make it back to our place, I would never drink again.

I turned to the left, and suddenly there were the steps to Yia-Yia's. I sat on them, looking at the flowers and sobbing. The door was ajar, and once I'd calmed down, I quietly tiptoed in, praying and hoping to find Karena in our sleeping quarters.

The fresh, white linens from the night before still covered the empty bed. She wasn't there!

There were bodies in all the other beds, though, meaning Stavros, Christophe, and Costa had made it back. I was so relieved to see them that I decided they probably knew where Karena had ended up. Exhausted, I quietly slithered myself between the linens of my bed. The mattress was hard, but it provided refuge to my broken self. I just needed to close my eyes and sleep. I told myself everything would be better when I woke up.

Stavros gently shook me awake. He was worried about Karena. Startled, I sat up and replied, "What do you mean? Wasn't she with you?"

"No. I left long before the both of you. The last I saw her she was with a crowd of Australians."

"Australians?" I thought back to the night before. I didn't remember speaking with anyone from Australia. Whom had Karena met?

Stavros said we needed to get ourselves ready soon; the ferry was leaving late that afternoon to make the trip back to Athens. I began to cry as I told him my tickets were gone. All my possessions had been stolen; I had no money. I had nothing. He smiled kindly and told me not to worry; this was precisely why Yia-Yia kept everyone's passport. He had lived on the island for most of his life and told me it was magic. Everything would work out, he promised.

But how could I not worry? My friend was missing, I had no money, and I needed to fly all the way to London. Stavros assured me they would find her and get her back to Athens. Again, how would she even know where to find me in Athens? He smiled again.

I decided to trust him. Talk about having a moment of faith—a moment of belief in something bigger than you, in which you trust in the divine universe, whatever that might be. My inner knowing told me there was so much larger and bigger than I and that if I continued to trust in it and speak to it, it would speak back to me. I knew that if I gave it all I had, it would give back to me. If I helped others, it would help me. I just knew. And I was right; that inner knowing is still with me today.

We waited until the last possible moment, but Karena didn't come. Stavros and I walked down to the port and boarded the ferry. Very few words were spoken. He just held my hand as a friend would, occasionally reassuring me that everything would be okay. It felt like the longest ferry ride ever—and actually, it may have been, because we had chosen the cheapest way back to Athens, so we stopped at many ports along the way. At each stop, some travelers boarded the ferry while others disembarked. A fresh, inspired look on their faces indicated that their journey was just beginning, while the weathered, worn travelers getting back to their home countries appeared exhausted. For the first time since that morning in Paris, I had no desire to speak with anyone.

I kept my head down most of the time. The sadness crept in. I tried to sort out the sequence of events in my mind. *What friend would just go off like that and leave me? Why wouldn't she show up on time for the prepurchased ferry tickets? Is this a joke?*

Was she even alive?

I had never felt so concerned about someone—or so mad. Stavros said she would catch the next ferry. He assured me that he had sent friends to search for her and that they would bring her back. If she was okay, I told myself, she really was the most irresponsible friend I'd ever had.

My eyes peeked from the Turkish cotton towel I used to protect my head from the sun. I glared into the sky and prayed again. I found myself praying for a friend who had betrayed me the evening before. I prayed harder.

Our ferry reached the port. We disembarked, and Stavros helped with my backpack. He had kindly arranged a well-kept room for me at a nearby hotel. I dreaded having to make the phone call back home. Stavros suggested that I have my parents wire money to the US embassy in London so that upon landing, I could take a taxi directly there. The US embassy would put us up in the University of London dormitories. He gave me enough money to get myself to the airport. In my mind, there was no way I was flying back to London without Karena; she would surely arrive before the flight. How would I explain to her parents that I had lost her and left her on an island alone—let alone flown to another country? Nothing made sense.

I took a hot shower. I sat. I prayed. Picking up the black phone in the hotel room to call my mother was the hardest thing I'd done at that point in my life. I was terrified to tell her I had failed at independence. The trip had been going so perfectly up until that point; I had only four days left, and they were supposed to be the best of all.

I explained about the stolen purse. My mother took it all in and told me she would wire the money.

I sat and wrote in my travel journal. Remarkably, I still have the entry today. When I look back, I see how I thought of myself in that moment: a fool for trusting the wrong person. Irresponsible, a failure, and alone.

Late that evening there was a knock at the door. I got up and opened it to find my Karena standing there with a crowd of Australians. They had gotten her back on the next ferry, even going so far as to purchase her ticket. Stavros had left the hostel address with Yia-Yia, which Karena received when she picked up her luggage. She was alive! As soon as that realization sank in, I wanted to kill her.

But Karena explained. She had fallen asleep underneath large boulders just off the beach with the Australians, enjoying the moonlit sky—the same moonlit sky I had been enjoying. Then she had been unable to find her way back through the white-washed maze to Yia-Yia's. Karena's story was pretty close to mine; she hadn't meant to abandon me any more than I had meant to abandon her. I thought about the two of us there under the same moon, on the same beach, in the vastness of such a dark place. In retrospect, reflecting on how little I'd had to drink and on how soundly I'd slept, I wonder whether our drinks were spiked—but I'll never know.

That night in Athens, all I cared about was that my friend was alive. I was also very much alive, and we had a flight out to London the next day.

Over thirty years later, the vision of myself I had that day is still deeply embedded in my soul. I realize now that it's time to let it go. I didn't fail; I persevered. I wasn't alone; I prayed to something higher, and I found solace in the voice that answered back. Neither Karena nor I was irresponsible in general; we just each made a mistake. And I may have trusted the wrong person when I fell asleep next to the guy from Toronto, but I turned right around and put my trust in someone who was fully worthy of it—Stavros—which ended up working out just fine.

This last piece was the hardest to swallow, because at that point in my life, I was in a dance between wanting to be independent and needing to ask for help. Looking back on my experience in Greece, I realize that the fact that I needed to depend on another in a challenging situation doesn't mean I had lost my independence. I spent years processing this experience, and what I've finally come to is this: We are all human. When a kindhearted person offers his or her assistance, it doesn't mean we are weak. In fact, sometimes accepting help makes us strong. I often witness people making their lives harder than they need to be by trying to be superheroes. I know I've certainly wasted a lot of time doing this. But the truth is that all the experiences we endure throughout our lifetimes shape us into who we are today—the experiences wherein we're independent as well as the ones wherein we ask for help.

The experience of having everything stolen from me while in a foreign land left me feeling powerless. At the time, I let this event limit me, even though I had plenty of resources at my fingertips. I didn't know yet how to become limitless in a powerless situation. I would have to face powerlessness several more times before I understood that only I could limit myself, regardless of what was happening in the world around me.

Questions for Reflection

1. Have you ever had to trust a stranger? How did that experience work out?

2. Have you ever made mistakes for which you haven't forgiven yourself?

3. What could you do today to surrender those mistakes to the divine?

Chapter 5

A Chance Meeting

For everything you have missed, you have gained something else, and for everything you gain, you lose something else.

—Ralph Waldo Emerson

After I returned home from my trip to Europe, I learned that Rick and his longtime girlfriend had broken up. Rick was seven years older than I. I'd felt like just a kid when I first met him. He seemed like so much more of an adult, with a beautiful, smart girlfriend. I'd thought he was going to marry her. But they were slowly growing apart, and every day I watched him become more and more frustrated about this fact. It appeared that frustration had come to its apex while I was on my European adventure.

Of course, I didn't hear this from Rick directly; he was a naturally secretive person, not one to air his dirty laundry all over the place. I felt his sadness but also a sense of relief. I tried not to pry, but during the two, long evenings when the store stayed open late, there were fewer customers coming through the door, and we started to talk. Sometimes he helped me with my college math homework. This led to some great conversations, and I eventually began calling him by his family's nickname, Ricky. We learned we both had late-May birthdays, just two days apart from each other (though there were quite a few years in between). After the store closed, he always walked me to my car.

At the time, I had never met a gentleman with such proper manners. I never really wanted to date anyone my age because most of the boys were very immature, and I hadn't found anyone who appealed to me. There was something very special about my boss. He had a twinkle in his eye and was always willing to please and help out. He seemed a bit intimidating on the outside, but once I was able to get to know him and engage in conversation, I found he was truly soft on the inside, like a marshmallow. I thoroughly enjoyed learning from him. He had a way of explaining things that helped me understand.

He was intelligent, and I felt as if I were working with a master teacher. It seemed that there wasn't a question he couldn't answer, and I was amazed that one person could know so much. His inquisitive mind opened up my sense of intrigue. I wanted to explore more of his personality.

The two nights a week we worked late and closed the store together gave us a chance to open up our conversations about our lives outside of work. It was interesting to learn more about him. I was surprised to find that he stayed to himself quite a bit; he usually went home alone, and he was a huge movie buff.

One Friday evening after work, I stopped by a movie rental store to browse the newest selections. While strolling the aisles, looking near the bottom row of movies, I recognized a man's shoes. I looked up to find Rick standing there, his eyes scanning the shelf. "Fancy meeting you here," I said.

He had a whimsical smirk on his face. The most adorable smile. He asked whether I'd found anything interesting. I told him I'd just started looking and asked how often he stopped at this location. He told me he was a regular and returned nearly every night. Hearing this, I thought he actually appeared a bit lonely and sad.

After engaging in some small talk and choosing my movie, I got in my car and began to drive. But I thought quite a bit about the coincidence of running into him at the movie rental store. I also ran his days through my mind, imagining him working all day long and going home to pop a movie into his VCR—alone.

Driving home through the darkness of the rural country roads that night, my mind wandered to what his life might be like on a day off. He was a great boss and kept his professionalism during work hours, but there was definitely something special about him that appealed to me.

I didn't really know what he thought of me. And I didn't learn until much later. After a long weekend, I was back to school and work on Monday. I arrived for my late-afternoon shift, and together Rick and I worked until close. I vacuumed the carpets while he counted the money in the cashier's drawer and cashed out after the day's sales.

In less than two weeks, I would be leaving the dance shop to work downtown. After returning from my European adventure, I had completed the last of my college courses. I was empowered and well on my way to true independence; I had already accepted a full-time position in my career field. I was excited to begin my career and earn more money, but I was also a bit sad to leave the job I was so passionate about.

We locked up the store and walked across the street to our cars in the wet, sleet-like snow. It was January 11, 1988, exactly six months after I'd left for Europe. Rick stopped and asked me, "Do you want to go out and get a drink? We can celebrate your new job."

It seemed like an odd idea; it was a Monday night. But I liked working with Rick and had never done anything with him after work. Perplexed, I nodded and said, "That sounds like a great idea."

It was a fifteen-minute drive downtown. We talked during the drive about how he liked to watch movies, and he spoke about his favorite actors. We also conversed about the new downtown building I would be working in, which had been under construction for several months. He wanted to drive by and see it.

I felt empowered and gave him a bit of insight of what my days would be like at my new, professional job. With a bit of nervousness, I pointed to the window that would be my office. I also pointed out where I would be parking my car. We discussed how much I would have to pay for monthly parking and where I would have lunch. He chuckled and said, "You're going to be living the big life now!"

I still didn't realize he had a soft spot for me and was having a difficult time letting go. In hindsight I see it was important to him to imagine me going about my day, and this concern remained true throughout my life.

He pulled into the cinema theater parking area. I thought this was even more strange; I didn't really see a place to get a drink.

"Would you like to see a movie?" he asked.

"Sure, that would be fun," I replied.

I was happy to realize that red Twizzlers and buttered popcorn were his favorites, just like me. We shared a bag of each. He generously paid for everything.

The movie we saw was *Planes, Trains and Automobiles*, starring Chevy Chase. It's still one of my favorites. I will never forget Rick's kind and respectful nature that evening. He reached out to hold my hand during the film, which reminded me of an old-fashioned love story—just like you would see in the movies. I think my nervousness showed. After all, he was still my boss, and I was much younger than he. But at the same time, neither of those things seemed to really matter.

There is a character in the movie named "Del," whose name became symbolic for us. Anytime either of us wanted to remember the special feelings we'd shared toward one another that night in the movie theater, we would simply say, "Del." Back at On Pointe Dance Shop, Rick had an old-fashioned desk blotter. In the upper right-hand corner, he drew a heart shape and wrote the word "Del" inside it. Every time I saw it, I thought back to that night when our secret romantic relationship began to blossom.

I remember the first time he drove out to my family home, down the long road past the cemetery. I first heard the sounds of the gravel crumbling beneath his '88 turquoise-blue Mercury Topaz as it slowly crept up my driveway. Our kitchen windows were perched open halfway to let the spring air blow in. My ears perked, and the jitters inside of my stomach made me leap across the kitchen floor to the garage door as I heard the ding of the door chimes that signaled he had opened the car door.

My older brother was on the wheeled floorboard underneath his '69 blue Chevy 396SS, talking to his best friend as they worked on the engine like usual. He took great pride in his beauty. When he wheeled his floorboard out from underneath the hood, the first thing he saw was a pair of size-eight cordovan Bass Weejun loafers. He then looked up to see Rick's golf-tanned ankles and argyle sweater. My brother slowly wiped his greasy hands on a shop towel and shook his head, wondering what this preppy boy was doing out in the country, and Rick never lost the nickname of Loafer Man.

I skipped down the driveway and leaped into the passenger side of the car, and off we went. I felt so proud to be escaping my rural life with an intelligent, mature man. He drove a nice, shiny new car. I, on the other hand, had driven only old cars. The freedom and excitement of driving away with him and going on a date left me gleaming with delight. I had never had a man pick me up at my house—it truly was a first—and this was a man of quality. The way he looked at me made me feel special. His confidence made me feel powerful. And his knowledge about the world made me feel as though we could conquer anything.

That first time he picked me up, he suddenly slowed down and pulled off to the side of the road in front of the cemetery. He motioned with his finger for me to look up. "Do you see that?" he asked. I looked up at the gray stone mausoleum engraved with his family's name. It was the largest burial stone I had ever seen. I was speechless.

Two weeks later I put on my best business suit with nylon stockings and high heels, grabbing my black, shiny, new briefcase on my way out the door. During the first day at my new job, I was sitting at the front reception desk when the elevator doors opened to reveal a delivery boy carrying the biggest bouquet of flowers I had ever seen, mostly filled with roses in a variety of colors. The card read, "I will miss your smile every day—good luck on your first day. Love, Ricky."

As it turned out, handwritten cards in beautiful envelopes and vases of flowers would arrive each week to my office. The staff would walk by and say, "Wow, you have quite the charmer!" I thought so, too. Our courtship was every young girl's dream, with endless thoughtfulness, delicious dinners, wine, handwritten love notes and flowers. It felt glamorous. What I didn't understand then was that Rick really didn't want me out of his sight. He was happy for me but bothered by how far away I was. While working for someone else, he couldn't control my daily routine or know what was happening in every given moment.

I worked downtown for about eighteen months, dating Rick the whole time. Finally, I had to come to terms with the fact that the cost of travel, monthly parking, and daily lunches was greater than what I was bringing in. Meanwhile, On Pointe was getting busier, and they needed more help at their second location. Rick proposed that I come back to work for him. At first, I didn't want to give up my start at a wonderful career. I loved the prestige that came with getting dressed each day and going to work for attorneys and big corporate finance officers. I was proud to spend my time in the class-A office space. But inside I knew my passion was for dance, and I truly missed servicing my customers. My relationship with Rick was growing deeper, and I thought it would be great to work together again. At the time, I felt empowered by Rick; I didn't see how he controlled and limited that power. I trusted that everything was going to be all right.

When we began dating, he was working hard to finish up his master of business administration degree. It was the beginning of his last semester. I was a fast, accurate typist, and I often helped him type his papers. There wasn't anything I wouldn't do for him. I see now that he reminded me of my grandfather in some ways. They had a lot of the same mannerisms; they both loved golf, and they were proud of their old-fashioned values. Rick took great care in how he dressed—which, as my brother loved to point out, was truly like a conservative preppy—but I found it very mature. I felt a great sense of freedom with him while he wined and dined me at small, intimate, expensive restaurants. He introduced me to nice wines, and I began to mark and date the corks. He seemed to always know the owner and staff at the restaurants, signaling to me that he was a regular. We were madly in love—head over heels—and could even finish each other's sentences. Somehow in all this I dismissed some early signs of controlling, obsessive behavior.

In the summer of 1991, we went to the Buffalo Memorial Auditorium to see Whitney Houston perform as part of her "I'm Your Baby Tonight" World Tour. We had been dating almost four years. Afterward, I just wanted to get home and get tucked in my bed, but he had other plans. He parked in front of one of our favorite intimate restaurants, where we were regulars. I was exhausted but still put on a smile. The restaurant was open late but still classy. It had red tablecloths and matching napkins the staff folded in a special way. I didn't have much of an appetite. He started by ordering our favorite bottle of wine—Louis Jadot-Beaujolais. The waiter poured two sparkling glasses. I sat and smiled at Rick's adoring, deep, dark-brown eyes. I noticed he seemed a bit jittery. Finally, he broke the silence by asking me, "Are you ready to grow up?"

What kind of question is that? I thought. But of course, I told him I was.

Still looking at me, he said slowly, "If you are ready to grow up, then put your napkin on your lap."

As I pulled the fancy folded red napkin off the table, a gorgeously wrapped, small box fell out, complete with a white ribbon. It was only then that I began to realize what was happening. I put the napkin on my lap and held the box as a shy grin spread across my face.

Rick's face had a soft, warm glow, and his smile filled the room. A single tear began to run down his face. With great excitement, he said, "Well, open it!"

The box held a gorgeous, sparkling, round one-carat diamond with our shared birthstones—emeralds—on either side. Rick got up from his chair, knelt down on one knee, and asked me whether I wanted to spend the rest of my life with him. I said yes. He asked me whether I could live a lifetime with his crazy family. This time I nodded as I said yes again. I didn't even realize that the whole restaurant staff surrounded us. I just kept nodding and saying yes.

My Loafer Man proposed to me on August 1, 1991. We married a little over a year later, in the fall of 1992.

Questions for Reflection

1. Have you ever lost yourself in love? Were you blinded by doing so?
2. What can you do today to forgive this partner?
3. What can you do today to forgive yourself for giving away your power?

Chapter 6

Dependent

Let all that you do be done in love.

—1 Corinthians 16:14 (NKJV)

September was our busiest season at On Pointe. The whole family worked seven days a week. Even after the last customer walked out the door, we had a long night of work ahead to prepare for the next day—the perks of working in a small family business.

When the calendar page flipped to October 1, we could take a deep breath. The busy times were winding down, and it was time to celebrate. Rick and I got married just a few weeks after the close of our busy season. It was a beautiful fall day with the leaves rustling outside in the light wind. On October 24, 1992, I married my Loafer Man, my Ricky, the man who completed all of me. I couldn't get enough of him, and he couldn't get enough of me—just like Barry White sang in our theme song, "Can't Get Enough of Your Love Baby."

We honeymooned in the most romantic place, the Amalfi Coast of Italy. Our flight to Rome left the day after our wedding. The country was fitting for our Italian heritage. The coast and the little town of Positano brought the peace and relaxation we needed. In many ways, our honeymoon was quite different from the European adventure I'd taken in 1987. Everything was new to me since I hadn't been to the Amalfi Coast before. After our busy season of work followed by all the prewedding parties and celebrating with two big Italian families, the small, quaint towns offered some quiet.

After a two-week holiday, we returned to the USA. We wanted to save our wedding present money, so we moved into Rick's bedroom at my new in-law's house. Yes, while newly married, we came back home to live with his parents. Now we all worked and lived together. In hindsight, maybe this wasn't such a great start for a new marriage, but they embraced us with all their love, and the Sunday supper table grew larger.

Shortly after our first Christmas and New Year's as a married couple, I learned I was expecting our first baby. It was now the beginning of 1993, and of course, my due date was in September—smack dab in the middle of our busiest season. My sister-in-law had given birth to a little boy just five days before our wedding in October, and Rick's parents were very excited to receive a second grandchild so soon after the first.

After the spring thaw, I began to look for our first home. We signed and closed on my birthday, May 28, and by Rick's May 30 birthday we started to move in.

With my five-month-pregnant belly, I carried all our wedding shower gifts down the stairs and out the door of my in-law's home. I loaded them by myself into my '87 blue Oldsmobile Cutlass Supreme. I couldn't be more excited to start our new life in our small Cape Cod-style house. The purchase of our first home moved me further away from feeling powerless.

We had a few months to settle in before our first baby was born. On Friday, September 17, 1993, we welcomed our darling little girl, Rose. She came into the world at seven pounds and seven ounces. As Rick stood at the bottom of the bed, with tears streaming down his face, he said, "I think I need a seven and seven."

A little over a year later, I delivered our second baby. On December 8, 1994, our dear son was born. We would call him "baby Rico." We had settled in pretty well, and my heart felt full, but we now had two babies in diapers. Rick left for work each morning while I stayed home to care for my two little loves. While my cup overflowed with joy, in the dead of the cold winter months, I quickly found myself getting lost within the four walls of our home.

At my six-week checkup after Rico was born, I complained of great fatigue. Of course, any new mother with a newborn and a fifteen-month-old running around would be fatigued. But this fatigue plagued me to the point that I lost focus in doing simple daily tasks. I had a hard time keeping up with the laundry, and just walking down the stairs and carrying the laundry basket back up again could make me collapse on the couch, where I'd stay for the rest of the day.

There on the couch, I read to Rose, pointing and sounding out each word while holding baby Rico. Our home soon became a disarray of bottles, diapers, toys, and a mess you wouldn't want to walk into. I went back to the doctor's office again. She ran a few blood tests, and I was diagnosed with Hashimoto's thyroiditis, and what was known then as an "all-in-the-head disease," fibromyalgia. This syndrome is well known and common now, but it wasn't in 1994, and it came with a lot of stigma.

The tears poured down my face in the doctor's office. I was shocked. I was a twenty-seven-year-old mother of two, and I really didn't know what I was going to do. We weren't making that much money, just enough to pay our mortgage and our regular bills. We had good health insurance, but it didn't cover alternative treatments. I didn't do well with prescribed medication and refused to take it. Everything made me more tired. I felt as though I were in a vicious cycle, whirling around and getting nowhere.

I was disconnected from myself and quite far from my limitless thinking mode. Limitless thinking is a constant positive internal thought process. It has nothing to do with our actual power in the circumstances around us. So even though everything appeared to be great, my internal self was screaming for a change.

I began to seek out some alternative therapies. I thought if I could relieve some of the pain and regain some clarity, I could climb my way out of this beast. I was able to get some temporary relief from a massage here and there, but that hurt, too. And we certainly didn't have the extra money to keep going. I also tried acupuncture. The treatments helped for a few days, but then I was right back to square one.

During the winter months I drove to a nearby shopping mall and walked with the babies in the stroller while I window-shopped. I was always exhausted by the time I got back home, and the three of us would need to nap together. I was fighting a battle, and I couldn't see an end in sight. In the meantime, Rick was coming and going from work, getting frustrated at every turn, trying to keep the house up, and seeking to make me happy. He didn't quite understand the fatigue or pain.

When spring came, he was happy that his golf season would begin. He was able to escape having to deal with my illness each day. I was happy that he had an outlet and encouraged him to go. He went off to the beautiful green fairways on Wednesday, Saturday, and Sunday mornings. This became his regular routine before heading off to work.

I did the best I could and plowed through. Our babies were growing, and their brilliant minds were developing. On the good side, through my pain and lack of clarity, I was still able to read to Rose and Rico. I read a lot of books to them. While Rico grew into a toddler, he began collecting all his sister's books and building huge towers with them. He designed the most incredible creations out of anything he could find in the house. He collected old cardboard, toys, and many small pieces. I often found my kitchenware built within his creations. He made incredible formations and tall sculptures.

Rico received a K'nex collection each birthday and Christmas. They were his favorite. He would sit for hours with the directions and put together large roller coasters, Ferris wheels, and hot rod cars.

Springtime gave me a chance to begin to think about my garden. This was where my passion lay; it was one of the things I had the most control over. I loved to plot out my vegetable beds and choose bright, colorful flowers to plant for the season.

Our marriage wasn't simple or easy, but we loved each other and kept on going. Despite the strain of being parents to two toddlers, we loved and respected one another. We never argued or raised our voices in front of our children. If we had a disagreement, we handled it behind closed doors. Rick was a very private person, and it would have been appalling to him if we had raised our voices in public. But it was quite an adjustment for me to move from the wide-open country space of my childhood to the city. We now had close, wonderful neighbors, but I felt very confined with the houses being just a few yards apart. I thought as long as I had my husband and our little family, I would get through it—and I did. But

I found myself longing for open space and a quiet neighborhood at the same time.

Through a good diet and regular exercise, I finally succeeded in getting the pain from my fibromyalgia under control. Eight years after Rico was born, I was able to get my thyroid levels balanced and became pregnant again. My dream of having three children came to fruition. The lovely spring season brought us a beautiful healthy boy, born March 15, 2002, we named Enzo.

After about a year, our house suddenly felt really small. The neighborhood we were living in so close to the city was quickly changing, too. My sisters-in-law had left the city and were living out in the suburbs, meaning we had to drive farther for play dates and such. I told Rick I wanted to move to a larger house and a good neighborhood for the children to grow up in, somewhere closer to family. We found a home in an adjoining neighborhood and moved in. I was sure our life would improve and get better. I was searching for a better lifestyle and a piece of something I didn't know was missing.

I quickly became the suburban housewife living in an older front-entrance colonial, complete with an in-ground pool and more garden space than I knew what to do with. I was excited about our new life and had high hopes and dreams for what I wanted it to look like. Rick just wanted me to be happy and healthy, so he was willing to do what he could. We quickly found ourselves financially overextended and in debt.

The strain was beginning to show as we tried to keep up with the daily maintenance of the house. The further away we got from managing the bills on time, the more controlling our marriage became. He began to question simple things like how much gas I used to drive around town and to monitor the mileage on my car. In retrospect, I don't know whether this was purely about the money or whether it was also so he could know where I was going. I also didn't have normal things like a debit card; I had to ask him for cash for every little event. Though I technically earned a paycheck, it was drawn, signed, and deposited by my husband, who was also my boss. I never saw it. I was used to this system; I didn't even find it strange.

I found myself bouncing in and out of this back-and-forth state between the dependence I saw as a natural part of marriage and the independence I longed to feel. How could I be taken care of yet still remain my independent self? Was this possible while remaining in a marriage? How do two people unite together and become one, as the Bible says, but remain themselves as well? Was I missing something? Or was I truly living in a very controlled relationship?

At the time, I asked myself these questions. I now know that many of these issues weren't inherent to marriage itself but were symptoms of being in a controlling marriage. I consciously chose to give my power up in my marriage only to find that it erratically grew out of control. My power was no longer a gift I was giving to my husband, Rick, but rather something he was taking—or at least it felt that way.

During those years in the suburbs, I continued to try being a good wife and mother by keeping up with whatever my husband requested of me. I honored and respected that he was working hard to take care of our family. Meanwhile, I lost touch with myself. I didn't disrespect him, but I felt completely stifled.

Questions for Reflection

1. Have you ever given up your power for the sake of others?
2. If so, how did you feel when that happened?
3. How did you or could you begin to take your power back?

Chapter 7

The Lack of Autonomy

Any action is often better than no action, especially if you
have been stuck in an unhappy situation for a long time. If it
is a mistake, at least you learn something, in which case it's no
longer a mistake. If you remain stuck, you learn nothing.

—Eckhart Tolle

Looking back, it was during these times that I finally came to
understand that staying married to Rick would keep me oppressed—
or at least *re*pressed. The framework of my ex-husband's life was
something out of the *Saturday Evening Post*. A regular Norman Rockwell
family. A portrait of a 1950s perfection. In contrast, I was basically Laura
Ingalls, wearing a calico-pattern home-sewn frock with a "made by Stella"
tag sewn in the back. And moving to the suburbs just highlighted all this.
The sprawling green fields that had held so much promise for me when I
was a little girl were alive with the same sounds of nature I'd heard during
my childhood. This land had strengthened my young soul by providing
me with limitless possibilities. Breathing in the fresh country air carried
with it a fearless sense of wonder. Though I still didn't know who I was,
I remembered who I had been.

Neither of us could have imagined how the subtle changes that came
with our move would be a catalyst that changed the rest of our lives. My
ex-husband's simplistic view of our life, although wonderful and full of

love, still left me wanting something more. I developed a hunger I wasn't sure of—one I knew I had tasted before but couldn't remember where. This was all subconscious, though; the day-to-day life of being part of my husband's family seemed absolutely fine, and there was no moment when I consciously identified this hunger and created a plan to feed it. It's only now that I realize this was the beginning of something greater.

Rick was an incredible man. Although his gifts came with restriction and discipline, he would have given me the world if he could have. He lived to make my dreams come true—as long as they matched his. And at first, they did. He supported me in purchasing the suburban house I wanted. He fathered three children with me, and I always had a new car to drive. But even though I was working full-time, I still had to ask him for lunch money, like a little girl asking her father for the extra change in his pocket to skip over to the candy store. This made me feel very dependent on him—powerless. I often found myself timid and scared to ask for cash, hoping he would smile and say yes. My soul begged for his validation. I was always trying to balance the internal me that wanted to live a limitless life with the external me who often found herself in powerless situations. I later learned this limitless way of thinking and living I crave is a constant internal thought process.

I felt the most freedom and sense of independence in my first marriage when I attended my weekly Mary Kay meetings. I will forever be grateful to my mother for introducing me to this fabulous company, which believed in the power of women. They trained women on how to stand on their own two feet and become financially independent, and that was powerful. It felt great when my pockets were filled with money I had earned. I felt validated as a person when I served my customers; it was a validation I had been starving for.

I truly admired Mary Kay Ash. Her motto of putting God first, family second, and career third resonated with me. Her rags-to-riches story inspired me; it easily wove into my ideas of limitless thinking. I strived to apply Mary Kay's passion for a product she truly believed in and the love and respect she showed to all those around her in my daily life. I followed these principles and applied them to my working life, which I shared with my husband and his family at On Pointe. At the same time, I took the experiences of what I had learned while watching my mother work in her own hair salon and applied them to my second job, selling skin care products to my growing customer base. I was passionate about making other women feel beautiful and happy to sell them skin care products I believed in.

At night, I packed up my orders for my clients. The next morning, I loaded them in my car and delivered them before going to my day job at On Pointe. I arranged morning drop-offs, and every week I held two appointments in the evenings after work. Every Saturday, I attended the Saturday-morning workshops scheduled at our training center—nearly always with a guest. Taking control of what I could control in my life removed the powerlessness I felt in my marriage. The independence I experienced by helping my clients and earning my own money made me feel limitless. For the first time, I was also able to meet a friend for lunch and not have to explain to Rick how I was going to pay for it. And I was proud to supplement the deficit in our bills.

Along with the perks of earning some of my own income, I was able to meet some positive, uplifting, empowered women. My mother and I enjoyed our circle of friends together. We were able to take summer trips in July to the annual seminars at Mary Kay's corporate headquarters in Dallas, Texas. This was a highlight of working hard all year long. The seminars were truly inspiring, demonstrating how I could live a limitless life by surrounding myself with likeminded folks. There truly was nothing more empowering than traveling with a bunch of women and staying in a hotel room for a week. I made many lifelong friendships at those seminars, and at the same time, I felt I was doing something positive for me and my family. I cherish the memories made with my mother, too; we both felt limitless when we were able to travel together without our husbands.

Back at the dance shop, I loved the products I was selling—pointe shoes, tap shoes, jazz shoes, leotards, tights, and fancy sequins to dress up the costumes. We had any apparel a customer could imagine for a dance class or performance, including hats, canes, and boas in all colors. It warmed my heart to meet their needs.

At On Pointe, Rick was an inspiration, too. "Treat your customers as you would treat yourself: With honor and respect. Serve them well, and they shall serve you," he used to say. I loved the man I worked side by side with for twenty years; I learned a lot from him. This brought me a sense of self-satisfaction when our customers walked out the door with a smile. I took great pride in my job and in him, too. We were building our nest egg for our children and their future. Our teamwork put the food on the table for our children. I was grateful for this.

I just didn't like the power dynamic between us.

I needed to be who I was. I just needed to be that person on my own as well as with him. I needed some freedom from the life that was so tightly entwined with his. I needed a little something that was just mine. At the time, I didn't even know what was wrong; something needed to change, but I couldn't see what it was. For instance, I didn't realize that if he went out and played eighteen rounds of golf, then I should get to do something equally beneficial for myself. I was happy for him that he was able to get away and have some time on his own. Why didn't I see that I needed the same? Our relationship was missing balance. While he was playing golf, I was taking the babies for walks and setting up playdates up with my nieces and nephews at my sister-in-law's house. We often came together to take our children to the playground, and later in the evening we all got together for dinner. My time was managed with caring for our children, keeping our home neat and organized, and making everyone else happy. That's all a mother should be, right? In hindsight, I should have taken up the weekly tap dancing class I saw advertised. I should have spent more time with my friends without our kids. I didn't make time for things like regular physical fitness or daily self-care.

It was as if Rick kept living his life, but I just stopped living mine and lived his instead. Imagine that every person on earth has this thing inside him or her—a love tank, if you will. Well, mine was running on empty. I did nothing to fill it; I stopped living out all the things in my heart. Unfortunately, nothing he did really filled my tank either. We loved each other, but we stopped filling this tank; I stopped reaching for my dreams and desires, and I don't think he even noticed. All this left me feeling powerless.

Then, when confronted with an opportunity to pour back into the relationship, I realized I had nothing to give. Fumes, that's all. I became a shell of a person. The life he gave me wasn't the life my soul longed for. He didn't know that; hell, I didn't know that at the time.

Rick loved me so much, yet I felt suffocated. He wanted the very best for me, but it was always his way. And eventually, our marriage became weaker, limited.

We existed like that for a long time.

Questions for Reflection

1. What could you do to bring more self-care into your life?
2. Where in your life are you feeling stuck?
3. What do you need to do to get unstuck, and how can you ask for it?

Chapter 8

The Affair

Being deeply loved by someone gives you strength,
while loving someone deeply gives you courage.

—Lao Tzu

Andrew was tall and mysterious. He stood looking through the window in my sunroom that overlooked the brightly colored spring poppies, which had just bloomed. Our spouses were in the kitchen, preparing wine and dessert. We had just returned from my birthday dinner.

"Aren't those the most spectacular-colored poppies you have ever seen? I was so excited to learn that we had such beauty in this garden," I said as I came into the room.

He looked at me, startled by my sudden arrival. "The beauty is standing in front of me." And suddenly, his alluring smile and deep eyes beamed into my soul. I was intrigued and a little shocked when his eyes wandered to my bosom.

The voices throughout the house became muffled in the distance as we stood there, enthralled with each other. Time stood still, and there was a spark of magic. Later, we would refer to this as our "Pixie Dust Moment."

Then I broke the silence, remembering what I'd come into the room to do. "Um … um … it's time for dessert."

The events of the weeks and months to follow were ignited that evening.

Andrew was born to an American-German father and German-born mother. He was raised in a German-speaking household but had become fluent in French while his family lived abroad for a brief time in his childhood. As an adult, he'd married and adopted three children, and he'd long held a position with a prominent international bank. I found all these details impressive. His intelligence and knowledge about the world captivated me.

We began to e-mail back and forth while he traveled the world that summer for business. At first, our conversations focused on the daily difficulties of our lives. As we grew closer, I was honored that I was the person he trusted to bring him out of the darkness and into the light. We grew and sustained our friendship while strengthening our mental and emotional relationship. But the attraction was undeniable.

Upon his return back to the USA that summer, we mutually agreed to secretly meet in a hotel room.

I eagerly awaited his arrival and was excited to learn of his adventures. Living vicariously through his world travel kept me captivated throughout the evening. We shared a Chinese take-out meal and a bottle of store-bought wine. And then he began to explore the depths of me. After months of filling my mental and emotional being, with great anticipation he slowly provided for my physical needs. The depths of my desires and a part of me I had never known existed opened up and flowed like a river. The experience of being loved this way was so emotionally uplifting that my body embarked on an unknown journey. The hours passed by, and it became difficult to part ways after this encounter, when our souls became one.

After he walked me to my car and shut the door, I watched in my rearview mirror as he walked around the back of my car to get into his. I sat with the tears flowing down my face, not ever wanting that night to end. Our cars met at the opposite stop signs, him having to turn right and me having to turn left. He sat there and paused for what seemed like a long time. I knew he didn't want to return to his darkness either. Without words, we knew a more powerful being had brought us together. We knew we would meet again.

After a few weeks, we started corresponding more and more. Then "Tantalizing Tuesday" became the norm, and I found myself having a full-fledged affair.

Yes, I was the lonely suburban housewife touched by a Fairy Dust Moment. Love hit me and Andrew hard. Real hard. The exhilaration that ran through my body and the excitement of something new were profound. Someone was actually hearing me, paying attention to my words, and filling my empty Swiss cheese holes with emotions I hadn't felt in a long time. I called him my "paramour."

Each time he traveled the world, he came back to share something new with me. His reflecting magnetism, lust, and adventure for travel immediately pulled me in. He bought me back to exploring my independent self on the islands of Greece. He brought out the buried part of me. With his eyes, he unlocked the parts a woman treasures deep within her soul. His confidence and knowledge about the world left me hungry for more. His alluring smile opened my heart; it was a vault of mystery.

In our hotel rooms on Tuesdays, I lay, anxiously waiting for my paramour to complete his work call. Each time he sat down at the edge of the bed and signaled for me to come toward him as he embraced my body. I quivered with nervousness and anticipation as his long arms wrapped around the small of my back and pulled me closer to him.

The minutes he held me felt like hours. He held me each time in a very loving way. I immediately felt secure. My body trembled while he took in the aroma of my freshly cleaned and creamed décolleté. My paramour loved the fragrance of the vanilla body cream I carefully smoothed on each Tuesday morning before meeting him, along with a soft spritz of L'Occitane's "Thé Vert." Mesmerized by my scent, he said hello to me each week in the same way.

As he disengaged himself from the busyness of the day's troubles, we both decompressed with a breath. Then he sat on the edge of the bed while I stood between his legs. We just stared at each other, thinking about how we'd arrived there at that moment.

Earlier in the day, I had wandered through the lingerie section at my favorite department store. I carefully walked around each floor display, scanning as I took in the beautiful fabrics and colors of the delicate, lacy bras with matching underwear in different styles. My fingers loved to caress each fabric as I walked through and imagined what my paramour would like and what he would feel as he took in the picturesque image of me wearing such a sexy garment. Each week I used my savings from my skin care business to purchase and wear beautifully crafted undergarments from my favorite designers such as Felina and La Perla. The colors changed frequently, and I always loved to mix them up by surprising him with a new look; each piece was beautiful and simply made me feel like a desirable woman.

In the end, I knew the issue wasn't about the lingerie or even what lay underneath it; it was the inside of my soul he desired.

Every Tuesday morning, as I began to prepare for our afternoon, the guilt of what I was about to do crept into my mind. At the same time, the exhilaration bolted through my body like lightning. I was now in charge of myself again. I felt powerful. I was able to make limitless choices. But I was afraid, too; I had begun to suspect that these limitless choices would come with very heavy consequences.

Tantalizing Tuesdays weren't purely physical. As a matter of fact, many Tuesdays were more conversation about life. Andrew was a good teacher. I quickly valued his patience and ability to speak in a way I understood everything. He educated me about finances and taught me how to read the stock pages in the news. Learning about the stock pages was something I had always wanted to know about, and finally having a grasp of the financial world around me was empowering, especially when I'd been coming from a reality where I worked full-time but had never seen my own paycheck.

One week he showed up with a flip chart, complete with a set of Expo markers and gray masking tape to tear off the sheets and hang them on the walls. When he came barreling through the hotel room door with all his supplies, I was stunned. I asked, "What is all of that? Are you bringing your work here?"

"Nope!" he replied. "We are having a business meeting today."

Andrew set up his flip chart in the corner of the room. He stood there in his business suit like the executive director ready to make a plan.

And suddenly, Tantalizing Tuesdays became more than an affair. He said he wanted to make a plan for our future. He wanted to discuss his feelings for me and what this meant. We both had families with children, and our affair couldn't continue as it was any longer. He told me we needed to either end this newfound romance or leave our marriages. We quickly knew we had to explore the second option; the questions were really just how and when.

My executive director stood there with his Expo markers, sorting out different timelines. We heavily questioned ourselves. He knew he wanted to spend the rest of his life with me, but I was incredibly nervous. On one hand, I knew that where I was in my current marriage couldn't be sustained for much longer; I was stifled and lonely inside, and I was ready to reclaim myself. On the other hand, I didn't know how any of this could possibly work.

Watching him write out different options on timing and how we could proceed forward made me sick to my stomach. The reality of this love affair was rising, and I knew I had to take a grand leap of faith here. But I also needed to trust that this was exactly what my paramour wanted, too.

We continued to map out a plan. We spoke at great length about how we felt for each other. I loved him dearly, and I liked that he didn't just love me back; he valued and respected me, too. I spoke from my heart, and he treasured every word. After a while, he sensed my nervousness and set his markers aside. He pulled the large white sheets off the walls one by one and rolled them up into a cardboard tube, saying, "That's enough planning for today." Then he stared into my eyes as he drew me closer to him. After he took in the aroma on my skin, he slowly began to peel away the layers of my soul. The part of me that hid within was released with each layer.

In choosing to be with Andrew, I had to confront my most deeply embedded feelings about living in the controlled environment of my marriage. These were emotions I had compressed and hidden within myself for years. The security I felt with him and his compassion to see and feel me as a powerful woman allowed me to release myself like an open dam. As we brought our bodies together that day, an interesting relationship developed between my emotional opening and our physical connection. His inquisitive nature for traveling the world was the same as his zest for exploring parts of my body. He became addicted to all I was: my smile, my laugh, my green eyes, and the curves of my body. I was the partner with whom he wanted to see the world. I was interested in what he wanted, too. Our hopes, dreams, and aspirations were one and the same. As he explored me, I gave myself to him completely. I felt the deepest erotic passion within his soul as he let go inside me, the tears rolling down my face.

I was like a dead, tight rosebud that had never experienced the sunlight. His erotic, compassionate nature allowed me to open and let myself go. It was powerful, and my internal self felt limitless.

The pages from the flip chart were safely stored in their cardboard tube, but I knew what my heart and body had decided. I just had to figure out how I was going to do it.

Questions for Reflection

1. What single, magical moment changed your life forever?
2. What's the hardest choice you ever had to make?
3. What would you do if you found yourself in this situation again? Would you make the same choice regardless of the consequences?

Chapter 9

The Truth Will Set You Free

Then you will know the truth and the truth will set you free.

—John 8:32 (NIV)

I had just laid my head down on the pillow that night, facing the window. The room was dark, and only the streetlight outside shined its brightness through the crack of the window shade.

Rick quietly whispered, "The truth will set you free."

My body froze as if I were in a horror film. The pit of my stomach formed a knot. The last few nights I had been extremely restless, and he had felt it. The tears began to flow out of my eyes and down my face.

He quietly whispered again, "The truth will set you free."

He knows. My throat felt dry and choked up. *Do I move? Speak? What do I do?* I wanted to get up and run, but I couldn't move.

I was approaching the fall of 2005. The leaves were rustling in the night wind that whirled between the homes on our suburban street.

My husband quietly slipped out of our bed. I heard his soft whispered voice speaking through tears in the adjacent room. "Do you love her?" My body trembled with nervousness. He had phoned my paramour, who was away on a business trip. It was three in the morning, and our secret was out. Rick knew I had been hiding the biggest secret, the most despicable act. I had broken the vow we made with God.

I was in the middle of an affair. I was on a wheel of lust and deceit.

As we faced the fallout from that night, Andrew and I had to call it quits for a few months. We had to stop, sit, and listen to ourselves. We both tried to focus on our current marriages to see whether we could repair the damage we had done, but all we felt was empty and incredibly saddened. Our two families were destroyed by what felt like front-page news. Since we lived in a small town, the gossip hit the grapevine and spread as rapidly as a forest fire. Andrew and his wife began to attend marriage counseling, and one of the requirements was cutting off contact with me completely. At the same time, I was shunned from our family, friends, and neighbors. Isolated, the consequences of my actions left me feeling completely powerless.

I returned to my daily regimen, distracting myself with regular household chores. I focused on driving my children to and from school each day, despite the judgmental looks, snide remarks, and eye rolling I endured from other parents. Our situation was complicated enough, and the judgments of outsiders made it far worse. When I didn't have to go out, I hid behind closed doors.

On numerous occasions, close family members tried to make sense of my mental and emotional state. I'd come home to find relatives sitting on our couch, ready to have a heart-to-heart chat with me. No one could understand how this sweet, innocent woman had found herself cheating on her husband with a married man. On one hand, I could barely understand it myself. On the other, I was trying to reclaim myself and my power; I was trying to take responsibility for what I'd done and make my own choices.

Our family managed to get through the holiday season. It was by no means easy. Then in early January I received a text message from my paramour. He was done with his marriage. He had walked away from his counseling session and refused to return. When the counselor suggested that he never speak to me again or, for that matter, even think about me, he replied that it would be like taking the oxygen out of the air he was breathing. He said he couldn't do that; he would be dead.

We told each other that over the months apart, neither of us could stop thinking about the life we had planned together. Even though we couldn't make any sense out of why we had been brought together like this, we both knew it was way beyond the point where we could go back. Either we would both divorce our partners and live separately, or we would explore the romance again to see whether it was something deeper than an affair.

He mentioned that he would be going to Brazil for several weeks, traveling for work, and asked whether I would join him. Immediately, the thought of getting on a plane and flying anywhere enlightened and ignited my soul. I really wasn't sure how in the world I was going to make it happen. I had never been to South America. I needed a new passport and a visa. I also didn't have any money.

Rick sensed that something was up; he knew me well enough to know by the look of delight on my face that something had changed. We had been quite distant with each other around the house, though we'd managed to stay amicable, rarely arguing and almost never doing so in front of the children. Despite how badly our marriage was going, we kept rolling through the day.

I sat down with him one evening and explained what Andrew had offered. Surprisingly, he encouraged me to go and explore what it was I was looking for in Brazil. He said I either needed to live it out or be finished with it—the "it" being us. We decided to keep our agreement between us and not to discuss the plan with his family or mine. He would take care of the children while I went off to find my lost self. I was going off on a mission to save my soul. I was dying inside, feeling stuck, and it was up to me to make a change. I have infinite respect for Rick for supporting that decision.

I see now that part of my being stuck was because an internal change needed to take place. I needed to be able to believe it was okay. The marriage wasn't working. I needed to release myself from it without hating myself. Slowly, I began to accept that what was going on was happening despite my best efforts and intentions. This realization helped me to get unstuck and was key to moving forward with my life.

Getting stuck and staying stuck can involve years of mixed-up priorities. It can indicate years of chaos that has been shoved under the bed and out of sight. By not addressing what's going on inside us, we often find ourselves stuck and feeling limited. But by simply rearranging our priorities, we can release the internal change needed to begin the external result. I saw my situation as a spiritual marker—the universe was pushing for me to change. Even though I felt like the door was closed, something was forcing me to look another way.

Within a few weeks, my luggage was packed for Rio de Janeiro. Thanks to my paramour, my passport and visa had arrived. I found that I was releasing myself internally and externally to grasp what my soul was desperately searching for, reclaiming myself and who I was meant to be.

My new chocolate-brown traveling suit with the colorful sash wrapped around my waist had me feeling pretty powerful. I felt independent again while I made my way to the airport gate. The excitement of the unknown and what lay ahead left me feeling limitless. A great part of me was saddened because I internally knew I was now on the brink of no return; my heart knew I would be leaving a relationship or a marriage, one or the other. The next week would uncover the truth about where I was meant to be.

It had been a long time since I traveled out of the country. So many things ran through my mind as I stared out the airplane window. I questioned myself but kept feeling the gentle push that this was what I needed to do. Once I landed and saw my paramour waiting for me at the gate, my edgy, nervous stomach began to relax. When I saw his smile, I knew I was going to be okay. A driver was waiting for us and loaded our bags into the open-air Jeep. On the drive to our hotel, the sun beamed down from the sky.

After Andrew and I checked in, the hotel staff took us for a tour of the facility. Exhausted from a long day of travel, we settled in quickly and unpacked our bags. We then lay down to rest and found ourselves waking to the sound of the ocean waves. I couldn't wait to put my bathing suit on and get out into the sunshine.

I never realized how committed I was to our adventure until my soul was submerged in the waves at Copacabana. Each powerful, crashing wave beat down the doors to the depths of me. I caught his eyes through the camera lens a few hundred feet away. He captured the moment when the door began to open my soul to the universe. It was then that I realized I was his freedom, too.

Day became night, and night became day. Behind the darkest curtains, the pure exhaustion of life overcame our withered bodies. While the sun rose in the early morning hours, our souls were still embedded in the darkest searching for life.

I was given a taste of what it felt like to be a partner and to be treated as an adult—as an equal. I was slowly emerging and had a sense that I was regaining my power. It was a direction I had longed for. Being able to make my own decisions about how I wanted to take on the day and communicating with another adult who shared the same interests were profound.

I learned that I had a voice again, that my opinion mattered. I was able to be part of the decision-making process on how we would go about our days ahead. Quite frankly, I had never been asked what I wanted or how I wanted to do it. I had always just been told, and I accepted. This new type of partnership was refreshing.

One afternoon we went out for a drink along Copacabana. My feet sank into the sand as I felt the sense of freedom in the air. I looked up, and a rush of excitement filled my body. I pointed up and shouted, "I want to do that!"

A tandem hang-gliding team was landing on the beach. Andrew looked at me. "You sure?" he asked.

I was sure.

The next morning the phone rang in our hotel room. We were given instructions to meet down in the lobby where a Jeep would pick us up. My paramour prepared his camera to take photos of me when I landed on the beach. It was really happening. I was going hang gliding. In Rio de Janeiro. I was going be taken to the very top of a mountain, and then I was going to run and jump off. It didn't even seem real.

Our driver brought us up to the launch site at the very top of the Tijuca National Park. My tandem partner got me all suited up and gave me instructions. He told me to run, run, run without stopping, right off the edge of the launching dock.

"Whatever you do, *do not stop*," he repeated. "Keep running." I nodded with great anticipation.

I ran, ran, ran. I didn't stop. Perhaps I haven't stopped since.

Finally, I was the butterfly. I was set free. I soared, beaming from ear to ear as I looked over the skyline and São Conrado Beach.

It was an effortless feeling of pure bliss. With the air lightly pushing against my face, flying through the lost space of nothing gave me a sense of everything. I had manifested and now released what was in my heart space. I regained my self-control. I was in charge of me again. Or was I? I wonder now whether it was really me in charge or whether the universe was pushing me down the path I was destining to be on, pushing me along to be with my soul partner and live out a future that was already written without our knowing.

I've always kept myself open to all possibilities, and the endless possibilities find me. They had truly found me when I landed on São Conrado Beach. For the first time in a long time, I was finally doing something for myself. There, on that beach, I decided I needed to live for myself in the rest of my life, too; instead of sacrificing everything to be a good wife and mother, I needed to take care of myself and my own needs, and doing so would make me a better wife and mother than I'd ever been before.

The experience was indescribable. I looked at my paramour, grinning. "Where else in the world can we do this?" I asked. "Are there other mountaintops?"

As we finished our week together in Rio, I felt as if I were living with purpose again. It had been a long time since I could make decisions without hesitation. I began to show Andrew the young, spirited girl who had traveled throughout Europe in 1987, full of determination, confidence, and courage. She had emerged once again. The experience felt fabulous. Embracing my feelings, wants, needs, and desires—and having them met became part of my daily self-care. It was a far cry from the automatic marriage I'd been living in, where I woke up and could barely get my hair combed and teeth brushed. Actually thinking about myself and having my opinion count, while respecting myself as a female human with dignity and pride, were uplifting.

I was falling deeply in love with being me again, and I was willing to share that me with this man, who treated me like an adult, like a partner.

Some people will never understand why I chose what I chose. Some people prefer to sabotage others, to point a finger and say disparagingly, "He or she did this." But I learned that to really dig within myself and feel the true essence of what emerging from within brought the greatest love I had ever found—self-love. Self-love is the ultimate source of spirit speaking from within. It was a true calling, and I answered. I listened and followed something without fully knowing what it was; it just felt like it was my path to follow. I fearlessly walked into the unknown, into the dark forest, guided only by an incredible energy force that lit me up. I didn't just fall in love with another man; I fell back in love with myself. In doing so, I found my sense of freedom to live from within again.

Of course, externally things became very complicated. Once I returned from Rio, I began heading in a direction I never thought I would find myself in. Despite it all, I took that grand leap of faith; I kept running right off the mountaintop. I leaped out of a life in which I'd had everything I wanted in the material realm. I had spent countless hours working hard and creating a beautiful family and a lovely home, but I wasn't happy. So I leaped into an unknown world, not knowing how or when I would land, just knowing I needed to feel free to find the happiness I was seeking.

I began the process of divorcing Rick. Divorce causes heartache for all families who go through it. We did the best we could, and I'm proud to say that our children are very well taken care of. I always stood by them, took care of them both financially and emotionally, and provided a roof over their heads. No matter what city, state, or country they had to fly to to see us, we always provided a safe place, a warm bed, and tons of hugs, love, and laughter.

Rick and I quickly learned it was difficult to endure a divorce as a single unit without all the outside influences getting involved. Everyone has an opinion. I find this so interesting. When two people join in marriage they become one; when they get divorced they become several. It's as if everyone in the community is getting divorced from you. I hear of this often when I learn of a couple getting a divorce. It is quite sad.

Sure, I was accused of lots of things, horrible words that threatened to tear me apart. If you listen to them long enough and carry those words with you, they can destroy your destiny. What I know now is that it's the unknown and others' fear of it that escalate these harsh words. Many folks simply don't have the facts, and others just enjoy the drama. I certainly never heard, "Hey, look at that mother. She turned a bad situation around, and now her children are thriving." That would be too easy, not nearly dramatic enough. They wouldn't have anything else to talk or gossip about; they wouldn't have a reason to call a friend and make up more tales and lies.

Following one of the strongest and most empowering moments of my life, I sank into one of the darkest times I've ever experienced. I internalized the gossip, believing many of the worst things people said about me while rejecting them at the same time. I came to think I deserved everything that came next—that though I'd had the courage to keep running off the mountain, perhaps all I deserved was to land on sharp rocks. In the many months it took to get divorced, it was often hard to accept that this was the new life I wanted, that I had asked for, that I had manifested. *Be careful what you wish for* was sitting at my doorstep.

Questions for Reflection

1. In what area of your life do you need to take a leap of faith?
2. How might people judge you if you did? How are these judgments fair or unfair?
3. Which judgments are you willing to accept to be yourself?

Chapter 10

Forgiveness

What I am looking for is not out there, it is in me.

—Helen Keller

The trickle of lukewarm water flowing out of the bathtub faucet and over my toes silenced my mind. I submerged my body beneath the bubbles while my thoughts wandered through my life like a filmstrip. Since my eyes were closed, I realized there was a pattern of control that went beyond anything I had done wrong. It wasn't anything I could fix. I realized I couldn't fix anyone; I couldn't fill his or her heart with happiness or fulfill his or her needs. And with that aha moment, I also realized I couldn't be dependent on anyone else for my happiness. Doing so would leave me feeling only vulnerable and powerless.

I am sure a good astrologer could elaborate on why this Pixie Dust Moment happened to me at thirty-seven years old. No, it wasn't a midlife crisis. It was my soul's contract longing for more—needing more, wanting more, feeling more.

It found me when I wasn't even looking. It opened up the caterpillar's jar, and the most beautifully, brightly colored butterfly emerged from the darkness of the cocoon. The cocoon had protected and provided security while I grew, developing strength and courage. But every butterfly needs to come out of her cocoon eventually.

And if we are lucky enough, we might catch a glimpse of her radiant beauty and her strength—the strength she didn't even know she would soon need. We might recognize her determination to land on every dying flower and bring a breath of air and life back to its root or the courage it takes to get ready for flight. Because that first flight is on brand-new wings, it's further than she ever imagined she could fly.

Perhaps we can even see her wisdom in understanding when, where, and why she was needed. And the *how*. The how she would get there in a timely manner. How she would survive and how she would help support the others when they were negative, weak, and frail.

I soon found myself like this butterfly. I had a mission. In flight, I understood now it was my time to give back, to repair the damage left behind, to wipe the tears of those saddened, to mend the broken hearts with hugs and love.

It was my time to emerge from the jar. It was my time to be their shining star.

I was a child from the country, brought up by a Polish father and a loving Italian mother, and I married my boss when I was twenty-five years old. As a married woman, I lived in a controlled, restrictive, conservative environment; and eventually I decided to leave. I am fortunate to have been loved dearly twice. I'm grateful for both of these loves. In very different ways, they shaped whom I became.

They gave me the strength and determination to be any and all I need to be today. Thank you, Richard, for setting me free … and thank you, Andrew, for catching the flutter.

I love you both. And I don't think many can say that about their ex-husband and husband without hurting either.

Through everything life has thrown at us, we worked together as a team. They say it takes a village to raise a family. We are a tribe. And I wouldn't want it to be any other way.

Thank you, Richard, for pushing me through the process of emergence and struggle. Like the caterpillar in the chrysalis, if you had forced or cut me out, I would have died. We each need to go through the process, as painful as it may be, for it was that process that filled all my Swiss cheese holes and made me whole again. Thank you for loving me, even when you wanted to hate me. Thank you.

I know I hurt you by leaving. I know you hurt me, too. I'm sorry, I'm grateful, and I forgive us both. I forgive all that has happened. I forgive all our weaknesses. I forgive.

Questions for Reflection

1. What situation in life has transformed you the most?
2. Who were the people most involved in this situation, either positively or negatively?
3. How can you thank these people for the role they played in your transformation?

Chapter 11

From Powerless to Limitless

The world needs to be inspired; they need to be given hope.

I have been dancing with powerlessness and limitlessness my whole life, but it wasn't until I went through these experiences that I began to understand what these words really meant.

Powerless means being devoid of strength or lacking the authority or capacity to act.

When we're powerful, most of us can recognize our emotional state and how our bodies feel. The world can be a powerful place. Certain people have powerful personalities. This is a very common feeling. Being put in a powerless place can even feel powerful when it doesn't limit us.

Writing this book has given me the opportunity to reflect on how certain situations and events in my life left me feeling powerless. It sheds light on how I reacted in powerless situations at different points in my life. Over time I learned to sit in powerlessness without letting the external situation limit how I felt internally. When I am in a constant state of positive thought, I am living a limitless life. Anytime my positive thought process begins to shift backward into a negative state, I am no longer living a life full of limitless possibilities. I have found that when I am living a true life of limitless possibilities, the doors open wider, and more opportunities present themselves. Allowing negative forces—people, thoughts, and so forth—into my space closes off larger opportunities.

I have learned that my inner experience trumps my exterior experience every time, and it's always within my power to shift it.

Walking away from a powerless situation wherein we limit ourselves leaves us with a lot of unprocessed emotions. This condition affects us in the long term, both mentally and physically. Eventually, one day we begin to feel the pain and sadness, but if we don't know what it is, it can manifest as all sorts of things. This can begin at a very young age when children are faced with anger or a power struggle at school. If they aren't given the proper tools of how to deal with this emotion, it can begin to take a toll on their confidence and social skills. As children, if we are lucky enough to be in an incredible social learning environment that teaches us to accept responsibility for ourselves and to stand up for what we know is right and or wrong, we are well on our way to a limitless future. When we give our children the proper tools to take a negative situation and turn it into a positive one, we give them the skills they need to face powerless situations, which they will inevitably need to deal with at some point.

It could be the man who has worked for a company for twenty-five years only to have his boss stomp down on him, claiming that corporate had to cut someone somewhere. It could be the housewife who has been in a marriage for fifteen or twenty years and opens her front door to find herself being served with divorce papers. It could be the neighbor who has just been diagnosed with a terminal illness. These are all examples of powerless positions. For a split second, we have all been there, in those moments when we stand there and say, "Now what? What just happened? What am I going to do?"

In 2007, when I was going through the divorce, my attorney told me it would take approximately ten years to pick up and move forward from all the grief and emotion I was holding. Living through a powerless situation took quite a toll on me; quite frankly it stripped me from myself. I went from powerless to limited right away. In the end, I found it was how I reacted toward the bitterness and reversed my thinking that made a difference. I found limitless possibilities, despite the powerless situation I was in.

It was important that I strived to find the right people to help me, even when I couldn't recognize the fact that I needed help. I never got those ten years to heal, rebuild, and move forward emotionally, mentally, or physically because within seven years of our divorce, my ex-husband was diagnosed with a terminal illness and died. A divorce is like a death. I lost him once, and then I lost him a second time.

We could forever be stuck in the past with the should-have, could-have, and would-have questions. Rick was the father of our three children; he was my first love and the husband with whom I spent nearly half of my life. He was my friend. We were very fortunate to be able to build an amicable relationship for our children, because we loved and chose to raise them together, even when we were no longer married.

We chose the format of how we would work together to make this happen. At first, the situation was pretty tense, but we knew that although we were no longer joined in one household, it didn't mean we weren't together for our children. I feel very sensitive about this, because it was exactly that; we made it our first priority to parent them together always. We made a conscious effort to meld our schedules together just as we melded our hearts when we created our children. We were both very committed to this. This isn't always the circumstance after a divorce; we were some of the lucky ones.

To the outside world, things didn't look so good. Not a lot of people could understand this; nor did they want to. It took me a lot of years to realize they were still caught up in their own fear. I could relate to that fear; in the powerlessness of divorce, I had a lot of it myself. I felt fear, anger, grief, and resentment. Financially, Rick still had the power, and before we found our rhythm as friends, I never knew what he was going to do next or what his next move would be. I saw the fear rise up in me.

The truth is, most of us fear anything that's off the beaten path. It is foreign and unknown to us. We make up all these stories and lies about what we fear, and then we share them with each other. This situation creates a fast-eating virus that runs through cities, states, countries, and the whole world until everyone is affected. This destructive virus just makes us feel even more powerless.

This happens in politics, as we have seen this past year. It happens in relationships, marriages, and dating. It happens among friends and colleagues. It's a fast-eating, vicious virus. Do we wrap ourselves in a bubble? How do we escape the nonsense? How do we choose to stay away from others who will drain our energy, being, or state of mind? Do we take on a nonchalant attitude? Do we answer back with "I am not going to discuss that now"?

I consider myself a pretty spiritual person, and throughout all that has been given to me in my lifetime thus far, I have always found that going back to my basic roots, honoring the values my parents instilled in me, and choosing to walk with God have helped me not to cave into the negativity. I don't let it take up space in my mind or heart. This is how I get out of fear and begin to find limitless possibilities again, regardless of how powerless I may be. This is what I had to do during the divorce and again when Richard became ill.

Questions for Reflection

1. In which situations have you found yourself powerless?
2. How were you able to access limitless thinking, even in your powerless situation?
3. How were you able to hold onto your positive mind-set, despite the opinions of others?

Chapter 12

The Leap of Faith

Miracles come in moments. Be ready and willing.

—Wayne Dyer

I surrendered. I gave it all back to God.

I felt a calling, and I followed it. I chose to live my life with purpose instead of living in agonizing falseness.

I stepped way out of my comfort zone, walking away from everything I thought I wanted and needed. And an amazing thing happened. A whole new world opened up. I followed a light that guided me home.

It wasn't pretty by any stretch; actually, it was quite ugly.

Every single thing I had worked on acquiring in my life was taken away from me. I lost all I had worked for—everything I spent my whole life attaining. Things.

Materialistic things. Lovable things. I lost everything.

To large extent, this was my choice. I left my marriage, but I didn't leave my family. In fact, I didn't even leave Rick; I left my relationship with him. Together, we decided that Rose, Rico, and Enzo would stay with him because he had the income to take care of them. I would now have nothing.

I gave up my home and my job at our family business. I hadn't been working on my Mary Kay business—the one thing that had been purely mine—for several years, so I had no source of income. I walked away from it all. My relationships with my friends and family were strained. No one understood, and I didn't expect them to. I was still struggling to find my way and understand what all this meant. I was taking life one day at a time.

Everything I had I had received from God, and at that moment I gave it all back.

When I had nothing is when I became something.

Because as it turned out, I did have a few things. I had hope and faith. I had something so much larger than me, directing my way forward. I had an inner compass, and I knew it was pointing to where I needed to be, even if I didn't know why I needed to be there.

From the outside, I now see that my decisions made no logical sense. My life was unfolding like a scene out of a movie. But I walked despite the dirt and disgust others hurled at me. This choice was really out of character for the sweet, bright, shy but trustworthy girl from the country.

One day after picking up my youngest son, Enzo, from preschool, I drove through the adjoining neighborhood to look for a rental house for Andrew and me. My paramour was now pretty much homeless; everything he owned had been packed up and left on his front lawn. As bad as things were between Rick and me, they were much worse between Andrew and his soon-to-be ex-wife.

Andrew and I needed to stay within the local town for the next two years, at the very least, so he could finish his volunteer membership for the local fire department. The plan was for me to co-parent with Rick while he worked and meditated on the fourteenth fairway. We needed to move close to make it convenient for him to pick up and drop off our children.

There were many days when I cried and questioned myself. I asked my paramour how long he thought it would take us to become financially secure again. With the strain of us both going through our respective divorces at the same time, he shook his head and replied, "It's temporary."

Temporary? I thought. *Well, that doesn't give me much of an answer.* In any case, we needed somewhere to live. So that day after preschool, with Enzo strapped into his car seat, I drove by a small bungalow on a busy road and knew it would have to do. It soon became our "temporary" home.

I had now taken the leap into the unknown.

The semitrucks whizzed by, horns honking all night, letting me know I was far from my country home. Then in the heavy, thick mess of two divorces, Andrew and I found out I was pregnant. He had adopted his first three children after being told he couldn't have any. I had three children I couldn't support financially. Our assets were frozen, and we were doing everything we could just to set up a home together. In 2006, the world was beginning to enter the recession, and Andrew worked in the banking industry. Neither of us was yet divorced, let alone married to each other, and yes, I was pregnant.

Soon I found myself standing in the welfare line, waiting for social services support. It was one of the lowest points in my life. I was filling out paperwork so I could receive food, milk, cheese, and cereal to feed my growing belly.

I remember the first time Rick came to get Enzo from the bungalow. Whenever we had the chance, we exchanged a few words. Even through the terrible, turbulent time whirling around us, we both managed to converse with one another. I explained to my soon-to-be ex-husband that where we were living would be temporary. I told him this was what Andrew had said. Rick was always full of words of wisdom; it seemed in my vulnerable moments that I was still seeking answers from him. I asked him what I had asked Andrew: "How long is temporary?"

"As long as it needs to be," he replied with great sensitivity and sadness in his eyes.

While I closed the door behind him, I peeked through the curtain and watched him drive off with our son. This same scene would repeat dozens of times over the next year, and each time tears flooded down my cheeks. The gut-wrenching pain and anguish in my heart clouded my mind. Again, I questioned myself. *What am I doing?* I'd had this inner knowing that I needed to step out of my comfort zone and follow my heart toward this crazy unknown destination, but all the while I wondered whether I was destroying my family.

I had traded the beloved days of gathering around the family table, celebrating a birthday or anniversary with pasta, meatballs, and vino (wine) for government-sponsored staple foods and solitude. The weakness slowly crept in. I found myself slipping through the cracks, losing a little bit more of myself each day. After Andrew left for the office each day, I was alone. For the first time in my life, it was just me.

Life wasn't easy, but in the isolation and lonely quiet of the day, I began to discover my true self. During the time of solitude, I regained my independence. I was able to see a future again. It would take many years of rebuilding one step at a time, but the process had begun, and it looked bright.

The switch was turned on, and the brilliance of the light bulb made my eyes squint. Others may have been looking at this as a huge loss and a slide down the ladder. I, however, sat reflecting back on my life. I thought about myself as an independent eighteen-year-old traveling on my own throughout Europe, making my own decisions. I thought about myself as a young woman who dated a wonderful, beautiful man who had swept me off my feet and wined and dined me.

He took me under his wing and made me his wife. He promised to take care of me for the rest of our life. I wholeheartedly accepted him. I said yes to all he needed and wanted me to be, and it became the new normal.

I had put myself aside for most of our marriage, only to find myself lost in a world of internal silence. But somehow I always managed to keep a smile on my face, thinking, *This is what I wanted. It's what I asked for.* Until I gave it up.

I sat in the bungalow, watching cars and trucks speed by for most of my pregnancy. I began to experience preterm labor and was put on bed rest at thirty-two weeks. Then, on October 31, 2006, I gave birth to a beautiful baby girl, Tilly. She certainly was a Halloween treat, arriving four weeks early.

At first, everything appeared to be fine, which was great news for a premature baby. She was born at a good birth weight and had a great Apgar score. But she was closely monitored in the Pediatric Intensive Care Unit because she had been born early, and she was experiencing low sugar levels. When a nurse first wheeled me into the Pediatric Intensive Care Unit, I had no idea what to expect. My previous pregnancies had been delivered at full term, and I wasn't prepared for all the extra beepers, buzzers, and cords attached to my newborn. She appeared much smaller under all the cords attached to her little body. The nurses placed a feeding tube in her nose, and her chest was covered with patches. All this was totally foreign to me. My heart sank.

I looked at our new little baby bundled with a pink cap on her head, thinking how blessed we were that she chose us to be her parents. At the same time, my soul searched for an answer as to what was ahead. The nurses encouraged us that she was doing very well, and she was strong. I hoped they were right.

I was in the hospital for a few days with her. Then, just as we were about to be released, the pediatrician came in to tell me Tilly had a heart murmur. She asked us to follow up with a pediatric cardiologist within four months. At this point, she didn't seem very alarmed and said it can be perfectly normal for some newborns. I was a bit concerned but not overly so; a close friend of mine had a daughter who'd had a heart murmur at birth, and the small holes had closed naturally as she grew. I thought perhaps Tilly would be the same.

Andrew, Tilly, and I came home and nestled into our bungalow. The older children were excited to come over and meet their new baby sister. The weather was rapidly changing from the glorious fall season and was now entering the chill of the November air. Andrew left early most mornings for work, leaving Tilly and me the entire day together to bond. I felt the love radiate from her, somehow soothing the pain I held in my heart for my lost marriage. The healing I received from this little being is indescribable. She brought me back to limitlessness. Although the external factors made me feel powerless, when I rocked her during the day and night, I felt as though I had everything.

In the darkest corners of my heart, loneliness was replaced with love—a forgiving love that radiated from this special newborn. The places where I'd held anger, fear, and resentment were filled with love and hope for a new beginning. She was my saving grace, coming into this world with a strong soul that shines brightly. She was magical.

Yet physically Tilly was facing a lot. There was something very different about the way she was developing. I asked the pediatrician repeatedly whether everything was all right, but they didn't seem as concerned as I was. I wondered whether her development was related to her heart murmur. Furthermore, I wanted to know why—why, when my other three children had been born healthy, this beautiful baby was struggling. As Tilly continued to develop differently than my other babies, I began to worry something was seriously wrong. Was the hole not healing? Furthermore, did she have a hole in her heart because I had a hole in mine? I felt guilty about the way I had treated Rick. I worried she was being punished because God didn't approve of the way she had been conceived.

Her needs and our financial situation forced me to spend time alone in a way I never had before. I isolated myself each day with this special gift. I felt as though there was a huge lesson for me to learn in that. When I did manage to get out to a grocery store or run a few errands, people stopped us and marveled at Tilly—more so than they ever had with my other children. There was just something very special about her everyone could see.

So despite my fears that she—we—were being punished by her physical challenges, I made the limitless choice to feel blessed instead. I only had to look to Tilly's light, and I found the hope and faith I needed to walk forward. It was time for me to let it all go and let God lead the way. I succumbed to face the fact that we indeed weren't in control; this was God's plan, and I was ready to follow him.

In making this choice, I began to see the blessing in my situation. Though on the outside it looked like I'd lost everything, I had in fact gained everything. I was beginning to find myself again. I had lost me years ago … and without me, I was nothing to anyone. The very things that made me powerless in that moment were in fact gifts to help me find limitlessness.

Without being surrounded by everything and everyone I thought I needed, I regained my clarity. Something remarkable happens when you sit in stillness. Surrounding myself with less, I was able to gain more in love. I grew as a mother. I was able to connect myself back to God.

I fell to my knees and prayed, shedding buckets of tears as I asked him to heal the newborn he had blessed us with.

And in the meantime, I took control of the little things over which

I did, in fact, have power. For instance, each morning in our rented bungalow, I wandered throughout the house, opening the shades. I simply allowed the natural light to shine brightly into my space. As I went on caring for our newborn each day, I continued to open the shades and let his light beam in. Sometimes it came through looking like a rainbow. This source of light each day was filled with the message I was seeking.

God's message.

God provides the backdrop; we just need to show up.

Every night I prayed down on my knees that God would heal and provide. Every morning I woke up and opened the shades. It was that simple. I just needed to show up and not hide myself in the ashes of shame.

Show up and let be, I heard. *Let go and let God. He will provide.* I was most grateful, and I began to live with a great sense of peace—just like Tilly.

Meanwhile, her physical troubles becoming more apparent. She had great difficulty feeding, she suffered from very bad reflux, and her muscles seemed weaker than those of my previous newborns. We attended our regular newborn office visits, and at the last routine visit I again expressed my concerns. There was a new pediatrician that day, and for the first time, I felt heard. He examined her records and handed me a referral slip for a pediatric cardiologist in our area.

As soon as we had that first cardiology visit, my slow and simple life grew much faster and more complicated. Tilly had an echocardiogram and an ultrasound, and the results came as a shock. Our baby was now in a critical state. She had a thickened heart valve along with two atrial septal defects and two ventricular septal defects. Her gradient was extremely high. They needed to schedule an emergency balloon catheter procedure to open her heart valve as soon as possible. We scheduled an appointment in Rochester, New York, where she could receive the care she needed.

Two days later we made the two-hour drive, and our baby was admitted for her surgical balloon catheter procedure. The procedure was scheduled to attempt to open her thickened heart valve. Unfortunately, it was a failed attempt. The image of the cardiologist's face as he came out of the surgical ward still haunts me in my dreams. He walked us into a small room and pulled up the radiologist photos to explain the problem.

He was very disappointed and said Tilly needed open-heart surgery as soon as possible; without it she wouldn't survive. After those words, I never heard anything else.

At nine months old, most newborns are approaching milestones like rolling over, sitting up, and even scooting around. Our baby was unable to do any of these things. The next few weeks, my heart and my whole being were filled with worry and anxiety. The unknown was fast approaching. My fear grew bigger as the days to her scheduled surgery grew nearer. There were very few people in our daily lives at this point; I had isolated myself from anyone I deemed to be negative, which at the time included most people. I didn't want them to creep into my new world with this precious baby, who was now fighting for her life. I phoned a few close family members to tell them about her condition, but their reactions seemed to be only great disappointment. No one knew what to say or how to even be there for us.

I had other reasons to isolate, too. I was afraid people would make the same connection between the literal hole in Tilly's heart and the metaphorical one in mine.

On July 24, 2007, Tilly was admitted to the pediatric cardiac unit at Golisano Children's Memorial Hospital for open-heart surgery. She was just a little under nine months old.

Nothing I'd experienced as a parent could prepare me for a moment like this. I could only continue to put my faith in God. While she was in surgery, I stayed the entire time in the chapel on my knees. I wrote and journaled. I asked God for forgiveness for all those I had hurt. I begged and pleaded with him that I would make better choices going forward, that I would continue to grow in my faith and be the best I could be. I promised to him that I would deliver any messages of faith he spoke through me to others if he would heal our baby.

The surgery took the entire day—at least, I think it did. I have blocked out so many memories from this part of my life due to fear that she would die, that she had been given to us and would be taken away so quickly. My mind was shut out from the rest of the world, and I could only hear all these words rattling around inside. None of them made any sense.

My parents comprised our support network at the time, and they were the only ones who came to be with us during the surgery. Andrew and I were flat broke. We will forever be grateful for generous support of the Ronald McDonald wing at the hospital, where they allowed us to stay in a comfortable, clean room the whole entire time Tilly was admitted; we were just a floor above her. There we were surrounded by other parents in the same situation. Some of these complete strangers we met in the dining area of the Ronald McDonald wing ended up giving us the most support during this traumatic time. Many parents had the same worried and anguished looks. Their child was critically ill or undergoing a similar surgery as our daughter. We found a common bond. Beyond that, none of them knew anything more about our situation besides that our baby was sick. They didn't know we were both still in the process of divorcing our former spouses, that we'd had an affair, or that we'd been financially comfortable and now had nothing. They just knew we needed support, and they gave it.

The well-known surgeon who performed Tilly's surgery finally came out of the surgical ward. He sat us down to explain the extensive work he had completed on our daughter. Then he diagnosed our nine-month-old baby with critical pulmonary valve stenosis. She underwent a successful surgical valvotomy, and the surgeon was also able to close the two atrial ventricular defects. But the surgeon also told us Tilly probably had more than just heart problems; he suspected she had Noonan syndrome. It would be a year before we could get a true confirmation because of the multiple blood transfusions she had to endure. Finally, she was diagnosed with a flipped gene mutation, the PTPN11, which results in Noonan syndrome.

To find the strength and faith to keep going, I had to trust. I had to know this was part of the path. I was in a completely powerless situation, but I refused to allow it to limit me.

Instead, I claimed it. I began doing as much research as possible to learn about our daughter. I wanted to know everything. My husband and I knew she was our gift; we would unwrap it every day and not know what we would be getting. But we were both willing to accept our gift graciously. There was something so very special about our child that was beyond anything we had even known yet.

Tilly's spirit is as big as the universe, and the wounded heart she came into this world with had to heal first so she could heal others. Over a decade later, this is still true. When she places her little hands on me, my worries melt away. Her spark and inner strength shine brightly. Her confidence and knowing of the world remind us of her old soul. We are truly blessed with our special girl.

We are fortunate that her heart was mended. As her heart mended, so did mine.

Questions for Reflection

1. When you feel powerless, do you think you're being punished for your choices in life?
2. How could you choose to see the situation differently?
3. How do you isolate yourself when you're suffering, and whom could you let in?

Chapter 13

The Choice

Travel early and travel often. Live abroad, if you can. Understand
cultures other than your own. As your understanding of
other cultures increases, your understanding of yourself
and your own culture will increase exponentially.

—Tom Freston

Eventually, Andrew and I were able to complete our respective
divorces and move forward with our financial lives. Then in 2008 the
world economy began to crash. We received word that everything in
the financial industry would change and that many jobs would fall by the
wayside. This posed a significant threat to our security only shortly after
we had finally gotten on our feet. Andrew always brought issues like this
to me to discuss—we were and are truly partners through and through.
As we mulled over a set of options, none of which looked too good, he
was offered a job abroad in London. The two of us mutually decided we
wanted to try to make it work.

We brought the issue to Rick and discussed how it would benefit
everyone from a financial standpoint. We also felt the move would
allow us to offer all the children an incredible opportunity to grow and
experience the world. Together, my ex-husband, current husband, and
I had a clear and serious discussion regarding our plans for Rose, Rico,
and Enzo. We wanted to provide them a world of opportunity, even if it

meant I had to make the biggest sacrifice of my life—moving a continent away from them.

The dictionary defines *sacrifice* as an act of giving up something valued for the sake of something else regarded as more important or worthy. My children were and continue to be the most important things in my life. I had to make a clear, conscious decision and trust that the gain was a far greater benefit than what we would be sacrificing. And the benefits were numerous. Accepting this offer overseas would help us as a family financially. It would provide a place where our minds would open to different cultures while exploring and learning about life through a multitude of travel experiences. This was by no means an easy decision. A lot of thought and many sleepless nights went into it. But I thought back to my decision to trust Stavros in Greece. I thought about running off the mountaintop in Brazil. I knew that no matter how afraid I was, it was time to take another leap of faith.

Before accepting the position to move abroad and join what is known as the "expat life"—working outside your home country and moving frequently from place to place—we had to take a corporate survey. It's a long process, similar to a job application or a personality test. It asks questions to determine whether you will be able to handle the great demands of living a new life in another country. For example, "Are you open to accepting another culture's lifestyle?" and "What would you do to mold yourself into the new surroundings that many would find challenging?" We accepted that over the next several years we could endure multiple moves and that the solid foundation and home-based lifestyle both Andrew and I had experienced as children weren't going to be an option for Tilly.

We took the job, and the first few months went well. But just under a year later, Andrew was offered an even better position in Paris. We knew this could happen, but we weren't expecting it so soon; plus, we had just found out we had another baby on the way. At the same time, the second move wasn't nearly as difficult. Believe it or not, it's fairly simple—if not easy—to move infants. It becomes more difficult to move when the children are older and have things like school routines and friendships to disrupt.

We were certainly up to the challenge. But it's not for everyone. Beyond the challenges the culture we had moved into presented, there were significant challenges associated with the culture we had left behind. We spent a large amount of time trying to keep relationships with those we had left behind. During Christmas and spring breaks, we went to the USA to be with the older kids when they were out of school. But I found I missed the American holidays in between these, such as the Fourth of July and Halloween, most of all.

After moving to Paris, I quickly submerged myself in weekly French classes and began attending a local French/English conversational meeting. The back-and-forth dialogue helped me to learn the fluency of holding a conversation in the French language. I also joined an expat family group and began to attend hosted activities. Raising a toddler and being pregnant, I looked back at the early years with Rose and Rico when I had been so isolated. I put a great deal of effort into making as many connections with other mothers as I could.

In the summer of 2009, there was a heat wave in Paris. It was one of the hottest summers the city had experienced in a long time. The air-conditioning we are privileged to have in America is nearly nonexistent in most European countries due to the cost of electricity and the historical buildings. Like my last pregnancy, this one came with some complications, and I soon found myself on strict bed rest for the remaining summer months. Desperate, I reached out to other expat families for help and guidance. I met some wonderful families, and we made strong bonds, some of which lasted all five years we lived in the country.

I was thrilled to find that many of them missed the American holidays, too. During our first summer in Paris, a local American family put together a party in their garden to celebrate the Fourth of July. Several families brought dishes to share. There were hot dogs, hamburgers, corn on the cob, and summer salads, making us feel as if we were at home and surrounded with American red, white, and blue.

But Paris came with its own pleasures—for instance, my all-time to-die-for dessert, *Ladurée Saint-Honoré rose framboise*. It's basically a puff pastry with whipped cream flavored with rose petals and fresh raspberries. My mouth is watering while I'm writing this. I loved picking up a freshly baked baguette from our local boulangerie to accompany our dinner too. It was simply *magnifique!*

Paris truly captured our hearts. Not everything was simple, modern, or convenient, but it had so much charm. I miss seeing the beauty of the adorned detail on the buildings and wandering through the arrondissements. The first summer was tough; I was on bed rest for sixteen weeks while Tilly toddled around the sweltering apartment. But the difficult pregnancy was worth it; on Friday, September 19, 2009, we welcomed a healthy baby girl, Bella. Bella was born at the American Hospital in Paris, France. She became our special Parisian baby.

Eventually, we moved out of the city to the small town of Le Vesinet. We still went to Paris frequently and especially to the Charles De Gaulle International Airport. When you are living abroad, there's nothing like having a reliable person to call on for airport transfers, especially for a busy family that frequently travels with an unusually large quantity of suitcases, such as we American carry. In Europe most of the cars are quite small, and it can take several to accommodate our large family and the excessive amount of nonsense we seem to need to carry with us at all times. In Le Vesinet, we met Sameer, who became not only our driver but also our considerate and compassionate friend. He was always available at a minute's notice, and he knew to have at least one, if not several, large vans available.

By the grace of God, we also hired an incredibly loving live-in nanny, Dima. Dima came with us from Paris to Le Vesinet to care for our two young girls. Dima is a unique, kind, sensitive soul, a mature being with an innate sense of knowing. I had never met anyone who had her confidence; she seemed to know what to do in all situations. She always stepped up to the plate for our family. When our older kids, other family, or friends came to visit, Dima gladly welcomed them with open arms. The love and compassion she held in her heart for others shined through. We miss her greatly every day. She kept our family organized, and boy do I ever credit her for arranging a date night for Andrew and me at least one a month—although she actually pushed for once a week.

Prior to this, I didn't know about the quality of life one could have when supported by hired help. Shifting our lifestyle made this possible, and it allowed me to have a very different experience when Tilly and Bella were young than I'd had with my first three. I was able to take an early afternoon off, sit at our local café alone, and journal my thoughts about expat life. I was reconnecting with myself in a different culture, and I loved every minute of it. Strolling through the exotic gardens and sitting on the lush green grass at our pond in Le Vesinet, I found the self-forgiveness I was searching for. I knew others were judging me for leaving my first three kids with Rick in our hometown, but in my mind, I was seeking a better, much improved quality of life for my family. I was choosing quality family time over a quantity of materialistic things that had left us feeling empty.

Life felt like I had dropped off the grid. I'd jumped across the ocean and was now living a quiet life in another country. I was learning about all the history while admiring all the famous artists' work I had been able to read about only in textbooks in the USA. Every day my mind encompassed more knowledge, culture, and picturesque views of historic neighborhoods and large cities instead of living a life dodging the neighbor's gossip in aisle 4B.

I escaped the everyday monotony of exaggerated stories and negative thought patterns, and I neglected the repetitive behaviors of ignorance. I wasn't interested in dragging myself down in others' thought processes.

We successfully continued to build a life for ourselves and found that living abroad as expats opened the gates to many lifelong friendships. We took in a lot of culture. It provided opportunities for growth for each member of the family. I loved taking the short countryside drive out to Giverny to experience Claude Monet's home and stand in the Clos Normand, the flower garden in front of the house that had inspired so much of his artwork. It especially fed my soul to watch the children skip through the garden and up over the famous green Japanese bridge adorning the lily pond. The family weekend afternoons we spent learning about all the famous artists from before our time certainly beat sitting in a classroom and looking at those same images in a textbook.

On longer weekends, when there was a school holiday, the Thalys speed train took us over to Amsterdam. We cherished that trip many times over and over. Studying the history of Anne Frank and touring the Anne Frank Museum left us all with many questions.

My vision of the world I wanted for my children came to fruition. I am most grateful and abundantly blessed that I made that leap across the pond.

I am aware that many others couldn't or failed to see my vision. And that is fine, for we are the only ones who must see our lives clearly. When the path is dark, we proceed anyway. We cannot let the fear of others stop us from succeeding. We may not always know where the dark my lead us, but isn't it best to try?

As a family, we had many opportunities to gather, from our summer travel to the children's school breaks and any other holiday we could hone in on. The time we had was purely quality time, and this is something I greatly miss from our years of living abroad. When we weren't traveling together on school holiday, my children and I used Skype and video chat often to stay connected. We did homework together after school hours over Skype. If their father wasn't home from work yet, as soon as the children came through the door, we turned on our "International Babysitting Service via Skype." This was a fun way to stay connected, listening to the stories of their school day and planning our next grand adventure together. We were committed to making this long-distance relationship work for all of us. Today I proudly say that we exceeded our expectations; I have three thriving young adult children.

Because of the limited Internet access while traveling on the European train line, my children weren't glued to their social media. There wasn't any cell phone usage, and no one was checking Facebook or Instagram posts. Hours spent traveling throughout Europe on the trains meant board game time or good old-fashioned coloring with crayons while communicating with one another through words and eye contact—things that unfortunately seem to be lost in many modern families.

We explored the ruins of Pompeii and walked for hours to discover the greatest old chapel or religious structure at the end of the road. We peeked our faces through the columns of the Colosseum in Rome by day and at night gathered around a paper-thin pizza topped with buffalo mozzarella, fresh basil, and authentic Italian tomatoes just picked from the garden. These memories adorn my heart with amore.

The summer of 2010 was spectacular. The day after my children completed their school year back in New York, they boarded a plane and flew to Paris—but not without my beloved best friend, Jenni. The universe works in many mysterious and amazing ways. That first summer in Paris, when I spent the summer in bed with my swelling belly, I really missed Rose, Rico, and Enzo. I began to search for a photographer who would be able to capture pictures of my entire family together once the new baby was born.

The next morning, I woke and was on my laptop, checking e-mails. Before we left the USA, we had moved our residence to Florida, purchasing a holiday home where we could all meet to make great holiday memories. I was scrolling through the page for our gated community there when I saw a photo of a family. I admired the photo and was wondering who had taken it when I realized the very house we had just purchased was blurred and far off in the background. I took the picture as a sign; I knew at that moment the photographer of that photo was my gal. I contacted the photographer—Jenni—online and set up a shoot for Christmas break when Andrew, the girls. and I would meet my older kids in Florida. We immediately bonded, and Jenni captured a most important photo shoot with baby Bella. Her unique talent for shooting and photo editing was incredible, and I knew I wanted her to capture all the other important moments for our family. We flew back to Paris after the holidays, and after a few e-mail exchanges, Jenni was on a flight to do another shoot. Jenni has become the sister I never had and the aunt to my children. We totally fell in love with her warm heart; it was as if God had sent her to us. Jenni has continued to capture all our family travels, taking photos at christenings, communions, confirmations, and everything in between. She has become more than our photographer; she has become a member of our family. God knows what he is doing, because in 2010, I didn't know how much we would need Jenni in the years to come.

We spent the summer of 2010 carrying around a large pile of passports as Andrew and I took Rose; Rico; Enzo; Tilly; Bella; Rose's friend Shelby; our nanny, Dima; and Jenni to travel around Europe. We had ten passports, ten airline tickets, ten ferry tickets, and a shitload of luggage. Off we went on the greatest family trip ever. Along the way Jenni captured all my best moments, such as falling into the Aegean against the red beach volcanic mountain backdrop. She brought out my fun, independent wild side through her camera lens. Sitting at the sea's edge while the sun was setting and listening to the click of the camera, my mind flashed back to the freedom I had felt on the shores of Rio.

We traveled to the Greek island of Santorini. A volcanic island, Santorini is one of the most gorgeous places I have visited. I hadn't been back to Athens or any of the Greek islands since that fated teenage trip in 1987. Returning as a family and embarking on a journey into the Aegean Sea were ones for the books. I loved seeing this holiday through the eyes of my children. Andrew has both an undergraduate degree and an extensive background in geology, and he was most excited to teach us what he knew about Nea Kameni, the caldera (volcanic crater) on Santorini. He had planned a full day's trip aboard a gorgeous wooden sailboat that would sail us into the Aegean and around the ancient volcano. Then in sultry hot island weather, the adults and older kids climbed to the top of Nea Kameni. It was quite a feat. I stopped at the halfway point, but the rest of the climbing crew made it to the highest elevation, and boy, did they get quite a view. The experience left a lasting impression. They told me their stories as we climbed down the winding, slated, rocky path and back to the boat, and I thought of my own independence at their age.

Later, we swam from the boat to the volcanic waters. Located at certain spots around the island, these areas are warm, similar to a hot spring. When the boat anchored, many people jumped off the boat to swim about eight hundred feet to where the water became warm. I was a bit anxious and stopped when I got to the edge; I wasn't going to go in. But Rico, my oldest son, was behind me, and before I knew it, he pushed me off. I fell about fifty feet and splashed into the cool, blue-green water. "Swim!" I heard. "Swim hard and fast."

I started to swim toward the hot spring; it was a long way, but as it turned out, it was worth the swim. The murky, orange muddy spring felt amazing on our skin. The experience I had with my children and husband that day was incredible. I'm so glad I went; I'm so glad Rico pushed me. My fear was beginning to set in, and I was going to stay on the boat. As we grow older, we tend to become a bit more cautious. I would have missed out on this incredible experience with my children had I stayed aboard. As I fell from the boat and hit the water, I had the same exhilarating feeling and energy that pushed up through my body when I was about to jump off the mountain in Rio de Janeiro. Jumping off a mountain and hang gliding thousands of feet in the air and vaulting off a boat into the Aegean Sea both reminded me to trust my abilities and strive forward despite my fear. Sometimes you just have to jump.

At the time, I didn't know the tragedy our future would hold. None of us did. Today I am grateful that my older children had this special journey and rigorous adventure with Andrew, whom they were starting to know and truly trust. That knowledge and trust would be called on much earlier than any of us thought.

In hindsight, the universe was building these unknown tight bonds between my children and the man who would be left to care for them emotionally, physically, and financially for the rest of their lives. Andrew would become the "fill-in," not the replacement, the very best person to care and look after our three children after Rick passed away. He would continue to teach them his wise words of wisdom and help steer them through the difficult road that would lie ahead for our children. If Rick and I hadn't managed to maintain some level of friendship, that trip would have never happened, and Rose, Rico, and Enzo wouldn't have had the opportunity to connect with Andrew before their father became sick.

Every child deserves a mother and a father. Not all get to have both. Connecting with Andrew has helped my older kids grow into the successful young adults they are today. Everything—the affair, the divorce, the shift into an expat life, Andrew's openness, and the relationship Rick and I maintained through it all—contributed to the well-being of our children. We tried to maintain a positive level of happiness and show them life was limitless, despite the powerless positions each of us was put in along the way. As it turned out, we were about to put that ethic to the test.

Questions for Reflection

1. What unconventional choices have you made in your life?

2. What did you learn about yourself by doing so?
3. When did stepping into the unknown turn out better than you imagined it could?

Chapter 14

The Call

When Life calls, you answer it.

—Louise Hay

In the late fall of 2011, we were working and living our dream, strolling along the river Seine, and taking in all the sights and smells of the Parisian streets. That's when the call came. At first, I heard only the concern in his voice; I didn't even comprehend the words but felt the fear. I heard, "I need you!"

Rick and I were committed to parenting our children together. Even though we were divorced and living four thousand miles apart, on two different continents with an ocean separating us, we vowed to our children to make this work. This meant using all the strength in our being. It required all the wisdom we'd gained throughout our lives to find the compassion we needed for each to support them emotionally, as a single unit, but we knew they deserved ultimate love and understanding. They deserved them.

When Rick phoned from his car, explaining to me that he was driving himself to the closest hospital emergency room, my heart immediately sank. Rick had never been sick before. He highly disliked hospitals, and he was the kind of person who wouldn't ask another person for fear of putting the other person out. When I asked what was wrong, he replied, "I don't know, but maybe it's my gallbladder." He parked his car and walked into the emergency room, checking himself in. A few hours later, I learned he would be undergoing emergency surgery that evening to have his gallbladder removed.

Our local hospital sat on the property right next to our youngest son's elementary school. Looking at the clock and counting back the hours, noting the time difference, I knew our youngest was still at school. Knowing our son's only parent and direct soul support in the United States of America was now in the emergency room didn't sit well with me.

That weekend, Rick phoned again. As the fear grew in his voice, I sat down and strained my ears to hear every detail of what he was trying to say. "They are doing a biopsy on what they have found."

"Found? What do you mean, found?" I replied. This is not a conversation you want to have when living four thousand miles away.

In the weeks that followed, Rick was sent for a multitude of tests. This isn't my story to write or my story to tell; it's his. And quite frankly, considering the private man he was, he probably wouldn't tell it. But the truth is that his diagnosis turned our world upside down. I can speak only of how it affected me and our family. And even with the ocean separating us, over the next few weeks I found myself filled with increased anticipation of the uncertainty of what was to come.

By the time he phoned again a few weeks later to say he had cancer, I didn't hesitate. "I am coming," I said. "I will be there." Soon I found myself packing multiple suitcases, my heavy heart about to embark on a journey into the unknown. Rick was still undergoing tests, and I wanted to be with my kids when he got the results.

The morning I first left Le Vesinet, I woke up in the cold, crisp December air. It gets very dark in this part of Europe during the winter months, the darkest I've ever experienced in my life. My alarm was ringing, and it was time to prepare for the journey.

I didn't know when I would be returning, and that didn't settle well with me. As I kissed and hugged everyone goodbye, I turned to look down the long walk through our garden to the big, black steel gates leading to the road. There sat Sameer, patiently waiting for me. Usually, I am very cheerful and have a big full smile when flying back to the USA, but this time I was somber. My husband walked me out to the gate. In his fluent French, he explained to Sameer why I was traveling alone. "Bonjour, madame," Sameer said, and somehow I managed to wish him the same. I stepped into the van, and my husband gave me a kiss. I jumped when the door shut; my nerves were a wreck, and we hadn't even pulled away from the curb yet.

We arrived with plenty of time for me to get my bags checked in. I was able to sit for a moment to enjoy my last *pain au chocolat* and cafe au lait, reminding me of my first morning in Paris all those years ago. I watched the people around me. When I am traveling solo, I become aware of many things I might not otherwise notice when tending to my family; I begin to experience the excitement on other faces. Looking at the smiles, I can only imagine their holiday time has just begun. Perhaps they are traveling to an exotic location or meeting with loved ones.

My mind wandered, thinking about last summer when ten of us had embarked on one of the most adventurous holidays we had ever planned.

It was now time to board. I'm not a good sleeper on long flights, and I was going to try to distract my mind by watching a few movies and reading. When I looked over the airplane wing into the sky, filled with soft, pillow-like clouds, life seemed so easy and simple. It seemed fresh, fair, and clean. I wondered how there could be so many bad things happening down there on land.

Flying across the vast space of ocean lying between our hearts, I landed on American soil on December 6, 2011, two days prior to our oldest son's seventeenth birthday. By the time the plane landed, the father of my three children had been diagnosed with stage-four cancer.

When Andrew and I made the choice in 2008 to explore new grounds abroad, we created a life full of adventure and abundance for our children. Living the expat life while working abroad brings enlightenment and cultural experiences. But when devastation hit my family, I knew it was time to sacrifice this lifestyle and put it aside. I made the choice to fly home to set up a safe haven for our children.

Rick and I found that under these extreme circumstances, we were able to pick right up where we had left off. The tense and careful friendship we had built up around our relationship as parents shifted into something closer to what it had been when we were married—not a romance but a close and supportive partnership. I was there to help him in any way he needed, and one of the things he needed most was the ability to solely focus on his illness. We discussed that I would stay and care for the children so he could begin his treatments during the day and care for them only on the weekends and afternoons when his health allowed. He needed to know that whenever he was admitted to the hospital, the children were under a safe, warm roof. I was there to provide love, support, and comfort for the long days ahead. We thought the situation would last only a few months. And even then, even after the stage-four diagnosis, some part of me still thought he would get better.

Questions for Reflection

1. When have you had to give something up to help someone else?
2. What did you gain when you truly gave from your heart?
3. How does it feel when you are giving to someone versus having something taken from you? How can you know the difference?

Chapter 15

Service

Do unto others as you would have them do unto you.

—Matthew 7:12 (NKJV)

Watching, waiting, and listening. Trying to find a bit of solitude while creating a space that was safe upon returning to my hometown, I immediately found some challenges. The warmth I was looking for didn't exist. I felt only fear, and my empathetic self picked up on the panic of those around me. Settling into the children's routines and gaining familiarity with their schedules were a challenge I was willing to accept. Rick didn't share his diagnosis with many people, but clearly something was very wrong, and the children knew it.

There was no one they needed more than their mother. I planned to rent a furnished townhome close to the children's schools. Being centrally located would ease the daily drop-off and pick-up times. Rose and Rico were attending the local high school, where they were heavily involved in after-school sports, and Enzo was still in his last year at the elementary school. With so many schedules, I worked to juggle them all without too much conflict; each day involved many drop-offs and pickups.

During the first six weeks, we were living at a nearby hotel. Although we had a small efficiency room, I was anxious to get everyone settled into a place we could call home for an unforeseen amount of time. I was connected to a local rental company, and I will be forever grateful for the woman who was the manager on duty. She was the first compassionate person I had interacted with upon arriving from that long-dreaded flight from Paris to New York. On my first visit to her, she had invited me into her office and asked whether I would like a coffee or tea. I felt as if I were back in Paris for a split second, where such hospitality is more common than it is in the USA. I imagine she sensed my exhaustion.

I hadn't slept during the whole flight; my mind was filled with nonstop worry, knowing I was facing the unknown. I broke out in tears from pure exhaustion, explaining my story. I mentioned to her that we would need temporary housing. Once again, like with the bungalow, temporary meant as long as it needed to be. She gave me a few addresses to go see. A few days later, when I picked Enzo up from school, he and I once again began the search for a rental. We found a suitable townhome with two bedrooms. I figured Rose could stay with me in the master, while Rico and Enzo shared the second bedroom.

It was the middle of January, and of course moving day brought in a huge snowstorm. Enzo and I packed our belongings from the hotel room the best we could. We wheeled and hauled two whole luggage carts down to the car, the cold sleet hitting our faces whenever we were exposed to it. It wasn't the ideal setting in which to move a family, but the excitement of finally having our own space and setting up their bedrooms kept our spirits alive.

Our apartment was on the second floor and had a balcony. Always wanting to look at the positive end of things, I envisioned adorning the balcony with lavish, brightly colored hanging flower baskets full of pansies, violas, and geraniums in the spring. What I hadn't envisioned was hauling suitcases and boxes up several flights of stairs in the snow. It was a long afternoon. We laughed and cried. Our frozen hands and toes were numb, but once we were finished, we gathered around the townhome's gas fireplace to thaw our faces and limbs.

After the first two weeks at the townhome, we quickly realized it was taking too long to get across town in the morning traffic, even though the schools were only a few miles away. We were cramped in the small space, which was a great improvement over the hotel room but still not fully comfortable. Rick was far less comfortable than any of us. After undergoing several chemotherapy treatments, he became a candidate for a major life-saving surgery at the local cancer institute. The surgeons would perform hyperthermic intraperitoneal chemotherapy (HIPEC). This is a life-threatening surgery that required a long hospital stay. Beyond that, the length of recovery was unknown. It was a stressful time full of unanswered questions. Stress and anxiety filled our lives as we tried to be on our toes and manage a world of uncertainty.

I did know one thing for sure: the size and configuration of the bedrooms in the townhome wouldn't work for us long term, and I needed to alter our plan. I phoned the rental office and explained our situation. Fortunately, they owned a sister complex, and another second-floor townhome had become available. It had three full bedrooms and two full bathrooms—but of course, at a much higher price. Well, it was going to be temporary, right? I said we would take it.

When I told Enzo, he looked at me like I was crazy. "Mama, we have to move again? It's the dead of winter!" I assured him we could do it. Even though it was a challenge, I was happier with the decision. This larger apartment was closer to Rick's home and very close to the high school. Rose and Rico could walk there if need be. The local grocery store was almost across the street, along with other shops and restaurants. It had the warm neighborhood feel my soul was longing for. It had much more light, which we would need in the dark days to come. With the bitter cold, I knew we would be spending a good amount of time indoors and needed a comfortable place.

We began to gather and pack up again. This time I was clearly able to prepare and purchase bedding for Rico's room, which had a large closet. Enzo was now able to have his own bedroom as well. The two boys shared a bathroom, which made getting ready in the morning hours easier. Rose and I had a large master bedroom with a full walk-in closet and an en suite bathroom. The kitchen was cute and charming, and there was a full laundry room—this was necessary because Rico's upcoming lacrosse season would require even more laundry than we were doing at the time.

My favorite part of this bigger townhome was the fireplace with the mantel. They brought the space together and made it feel like a home.

The place was cozy and kept us warm on those cold winter days and nights. Also, when springtime came, we could sit out on the balcony, which overlooked a tree-lined forest. There is something about the color of green against the sky that brightens even the cloudiest of days.

As we were getting ready to move into the newer place, my cousin Thelma phoned. She was getting out of work early and asked whether we needed help with anything. I explained the situation and said we were moving to new digs. She laughed and said, "Louise, only you." Thelma loved to call me Louise. "What is the address, Louise? I'll meet you there at your new digs." I was so grateful for her help. I'd nearly forgotten what it was like to have so much of my extended family nearby.

The truth was that since I had arrived, not many people had offered to help. There wasn't anyone laying out the red carpet for us. Most people I ran into still seemed to be mourning our divorce seven years before. Of course, I wasn't there for applause; I was there to take care of our three children during a trying time. I wanted to support Rick, too, who was undergoing chemotherapy treatments and multiple surgeries while he fought hard for his life. I told myself I needed to remain the optimist and keep everything running smoothly for Rose, Rico, and Enzo while Rick got better. The kids needed to concentrate on their school academics, and Rick needed to focus on his health. The most important thing was trying to keep everything as it had been before their father's diagnosis.

Instead of letting myself feel hurt by the rejection I'd felt from my former friends and neighbors, I told myself that most of them didn't even know what we were going through. And it was true—Rick hadn't told many people, and everything was pretty hush hush around town. I had no idea what we were all about to endure, and what I expected to last only a few months continued on for two more years. Because of the complex nature of relationships between family members and the uncertainty of the extent of his disease, our children and I were robbed of the truth. Rick was a great protector, and he never told us how sick he really was; like with my grandfather, I didn't learn he was dying until right before it happened.

In the meantime, I spent time connecting with people immediately around me. Rick's illness brought our children and me much closer together, and it gave them lifelong connections with school friends, who supported them through it all. I also established close relationships with Rose and Rico's friends—relationships I otherwise would have missed out on due to living abroad in Europe. Our rented home, just around the block from the high school, became a safe haven for so many to come and rest their minds after an otherwise-hard day. I always tried to make sure we had some food on hand. Teenagers often stopped by for a rest or an afternoon snack before sports practice. They reminded me of my own teenage years; though we'd been out in the country, my father had raised me with an open-door policy. He taught me to create a warm home where kids could stop in, take a break, grab a snack and a drink, and leave with a smile and a hug.

Meanwhile, Andrew was in Paris, caring for our two little girls, who were rapidly growing. Thank goodness for all the video chat sessions and the exchange of pictures. I was grateful that Dima captured the best video footage during daylight hours. This kept us going at both sides of the pond. We might have been separated by the big ocean between us, but our hearts were bound as one. Our minds were connected, and we had a short- and long-term plan. We took life one day at a time.

I managed to see them in person, too, on many international trips. My cousin Thelma helped with the kids in New York, when I'd fly back to Paris for extended weekends. It was a respite to return home to my loves, who were waiting for me, and vice versa; it was a truly remarkable time that required great strength, endurance, and courage to keep going. God had to be behind this feat. Looking back now, I see I was running on autopilot for sure, trying to be everything to everyone. But I'd signed up for it. It was my calling. *So this is life*, I figured; it was up to me to deal with what I'd been given. I accepted the situation with gratitude.

I was particularly grateful for Andrew's love and support. He selflessly gave and understood the importance of our being there for all our children. And somehow, we made it happen.

Conditions certainly weren't easy. When I returned back to New York from my long flights, I spent the day resting while the kids were at school, surrounding myself with an internal world of silence. I wept day and night for my children—mostly nights when the crisp, cold air of winter crept inside the apartment. I often lay listening to the howling wind, silently weeping, and praying that the night sky would bring a white blanket of snow with the early morning sun and that school would be canceled. I looked forward to staying snuggled beneath my bedcovers and cuddling with my children all day long.

Many times my late-night prayers weren't answered; I'd wake up to sunshine and dry, clear roads. When that happened, I knew I needed to wipe my tears and dig deep inside myself to offer a warm morning smile. I would try to clear the lump from my throat and swollen, crusted-over eyes from the tears shed during the night, wash my face, and prepare for another day. I'd throw a long North Face coat, scarf, and gloves on over my pajamas to drop the kids off at school, then crawl back into my bed, still warm.

But other times, the snow came, school was off, and we didn't need to return to normal life. In the early-morning hours, a school-wide text message came up on my phone to inform us that the roads were slick with ice and that driving would be treacherous. I rose from my covers and pulled back the curtain to find the trees covered in a glistening, white snow. The brightest of the sun's rays gleamed through the tree branches, bringing a sense of relief and new hope.

We loved snow days. They eased the pain and emotion we were all going through, along with the fear of the unknown, the words not being spoken, and the rawness of it all. The thought of staying indoors and sipping hot mugs full of hot chocolate topped with whipped cream while we watched a great Christmas classic warmed my heart.

I think I needed these days off as much as the kids did. I didn't want to rush out anywhere. I didn't want to be alone all day to think about the worst, and my heart ached for the man I once knew. He was no longer able to convince me that everything was going to be okay. He was no longer the man I had felt the most secure with; he was a shell of himself.

The deadly disease wrestling around inside him took away the innocence of our lives, the ones we had known. The warmth of his smile was gone, and the sparkle in his deep, dark-brown eyes had dulled. He had become a victim of a disease he couldn't control. My ex-husband was a man who was always in control every day. He was in control of himself, his work, and our family. For twenty years, he had been in control of my being.

But that was all gone.

The journey wasn't easy. It came with so many daily internal and external struggles. It was challenging on both sides; life in Buffalo was hard, and leaving my husband and two little ones back in Paris was hard, too. And yet the choice itself was one of the easiest ever. I would never turn my back on the love we have for our children. I would never turn my back on the one I had loved and cherished for over twenty years of my life. We were forever connected in our souls. We didn't need words to say it; the simple glances and tears in the depth of his eyes were enough.

And somehow we continued to make fond memories in our temporary townhome. From football Sundays to Fantasy Football leagues, everyone brought snacks and platters of food to share. There were truly so many memories during this time of the unknown. I am forever grateful for my children's tribe who came to support them and me. They always stopped over and had a smile and positive attitude to cheer me. My daughter's friends loved to hang out with a bowl of popcorn and a movie if I needed it. Those are the moments I will remember forever: the good times we had.

The apartment had a gorgeous view. The payoff was that it was on the second floor; walking up all sixteen carpeted stairs with a load of full grocery bags is one memory I would like to soon forget. Many cans fell through broken bags and clunked down to the bottom.

Andrew and I worked hard to make a long-distance relationship work. We made the best choices and decisions we could to remain together during this difficult time. He became my cheerleader. Every Friday he sent me flowers, filled with words of encouragement. He even sometimes flew in with the girls and stayed for an extended weekend. He went out of his way to get our youngest son, Enzo, in to see his father during critical hours. No matter what the circumstance, Andrew was always the guy who said, "Yes, we can do it! We will find a way." He never faltered. He was there for us no matter what.

On Rick's better days between treatments, the kids stayed with him. He loved to boil a pot of hot water and prepare some pasta for them.

This gave him a chance to regain some sense of normalcy in his life. I respected this and counted the days until his next round of treatment when he would need me again. In the meantime, I'd catch a flight back to Paris to spend some quality time with my family there. I bounced back and forth like this, trying to maintain as strong of a relationship with Andrew, Tilly, and Bella as I had with Rick, Rose, Rico, and Enzo.

I try not to look back with regret, because I cannot change any of it. We all did the best we could under the circumstances. The one thing I wish we had done was come together and talk more about what Rick wanted for the children—how he wanted them to be raised moving forward. I only knew he was consciously passing the baton to Andrew, knowing this man would end up helping raise his kids. I assumed he and I rarely had these conversations because it was too painful. He didn't ever want to leave us. As it turned out, he was having these talks with Andrew.

In the end, it may not even matter, because one thing I know for sure about parenting is that it's not a path either of us could carve out for them, even if he were sitting right next to me. This is life. I thought we could plan, direct, and educate our children to live out the dreams we have for them. But the truth is that when they reach the age when they can decide their own life path, it is up to them to walk it. When that happens, all our planning and redirecting go out the window, and all we have is our love. We can only hope we have given them all life's tools to go out and make good in the world.

When he was sick, Rick was adamant that he didn't want his illness to be the reason for anyone to stop his or her journey. He insisted that Rose, Rico, and Enzo keep on keeping on. They weren't allowed to skip school or quit anything; they had to keep going. I still have mixed feelings about this decision, but it was what he wanted. We were in clear agreement that we had to keep the kids moving in a positive direction.

The courage, strength, and dignity my ex-husband demonstrated during this devastating time in his life set a profound example of a man's mental strength over the failing part of his body. His fierce and extremely determined attitude to fight this beast raging throughout his body was evident. He wasn't ever going to give in to the weakness that tried to take him over. His mind was strong. I learned, watched, and witnessed an incredible amount of determination and saw that mind over body is fully real. He lived with a cancerous disease that should have killed him within months, but he survived two years and five months after his diagnosis.

Somehow, we survived those two years and five months, too.

Questions for Reflection

1. What is the hardest thing you have endured in your life?
2. How did you make it through it?
3. What sustained you as you did so?

Chapter 16

Loved Ones

*E*ach time I flew back and forth from Buffalo to Paris, I arrived home to find my ex-husband curled up on the couch, recovering from his last treatment or procedure. He was always getting better. Just getting better. One day, I saw something different.

It was the blanket I saw when I walked into his room that lit the light bulb in my head. I was standing over a frail, sick man.

That same cotton blanket adorned with a soft rose had been laid over me ten years before in the labor and delivery room while I anxiously awaited the arrival of our third child. It was the weight of the blanket and the softness of its cotton I remembered most. It wasn't too hot, and it wasn't too thin; it was just perfect. The blanket came home with me, as did the beautiful baby boy. It kept me warm and brought a sense of safety during the dark and lonely hours that night sometimes brings.

Now, ten years later, I stood over a man who had once given me a great sense of security and realized the blanket was there to accompany him, too—not through bringing new life but through bringing death itself. Was it bringing him the same warmth and security it had brought me? Did it have the proper weight to help his frail body feel safe? I stood in wonder, watching him speak as he tried to deliver a message, but I couldn't hear him; I was thinking only about how that blanket made him feel.

There were two completely different lives now, in the vastness of space and memory, sharing the same blanket rose. It amazes me what one piece of cloth can hold.

We gathered at the cemetery.

Some said a prayer, and others shed tears. We all had our part. One man's cancer had affected all of us on so many different levels. Each of us has his or her own story to tell. Each of us has his or her own grief.

Throughout the service, my mind wandered throughout the crowd and beyond the green valley behind the rows of mourners who had gathered in the early morning sun. Thoughts raced through my mind. *How will we go on from here? How will this great loss change us all?* I had never felt so much anguish for my children. They had truly been robbed of time.

The grief I felt for them brought back memories of losing my grandfather. I had been nineteen then, the same age my son Rico had been when his father died. I looked at his emptiness and felt his loss. I looked at all my children. They were in utter shock and disbelief.

I wanted only to be their mother bear. I wanted to wrap my arms around them, keep them secure, and let them know I was there to protect them with all my might. But I knew there was nothing I could offer them to fill the void of loss the following days, weeks, months, and years would bring.

It has been a lifetime since the loss of my grandfather. A loss Rick filled for me—I see that now. And now that Rick is gone, there is no one to fill the role. That heart space remains empty. I long for my grandfather's words of wisdom just as I long to hear Rick's candid advice. I long to be the little girl who stood on my grandfather's shoes while he taught me the two-step. After I lost my grandfather, Rick continued to teach me new things throughout my life. Now he was finally teaching me to grieve.

These were the thoughts that whirled through my mind as I tried to console my children. I realized how hard life would be down the road as they faced each milestone. After the loss they suffered today, their lives would never be the same. There would be weeks, months, or years before they would even begin to accept the true impact of their loss. Here I was, decades after the loss of my grandfather, finally realizing what he'd meant to me.

I could be there for them only when grief threw them to the ground.

I stood with our three children and watched as his casket was lowered into the ground. The sounds—the jarring, grating scrape of the shovel going into the dirt and then the thud of death as the dirt hit the top of the casket—still haunt me.

As the mourners gave their condolences and last goodbyes, I shook inside with a flood of memories. Not one single person standing here would ever know how my heart cherished that first date or how much this sacred ground meant to me. We were going to be buried here together. That was the plan.

Had all that been ruined because I followed a moment of passion? Because I had been sprinkled by the Pixie Dust Moment? All I'd wanted was to have control of myself and who I was meant to be. I wanted to take care of my family and enjoy my children. I became the yes wife until I was barely breathing. My inside was dying off slowly. It's a common situation, and I managed to get out of it. But at what cost?

As I turned to walk back to our car with the mourners, ten-year-old Enzo ran up and took my hand. Looking up, he said, "Mama, can we go home now?" I replied that yes, we could, with tears streaming down my face.

The years are passing by quickly now. There are still moments when my grief is in the present tense, acute. I hear others trying to say life will get better, but in those moments, it doesn't; it becomes rawer and more difficult. My heart hurts, and my soul is lost. I would like to think I am healing. But at any point, an event can trigger an emotion I thought I had buried so deeply.

When I'm deep in grief, I often look out into the sea. It appears to be calm like the night sky. But as I watch, a small ripple gathers up its strength, turning to a wave that crashes against the shore. In the same way, what I feel appears to be calm, but it rages throughout my chest and my throat. Then my eyes begin to well up with tears, and it's like I can't breathe. I want to feel, but I want to hide. I want to speak, but I can't talk. The situation is terrifying.

I feel Rick slipping further away from us, while at the same time his energy and spirit are so close. It's difficult even to walk without him in my life.

I want to ask, *When can we see you again? Will we embrace as we once did? Are the love and friendship we shared forever gone from this plane? Remember us always, and we will forever hold you in our hearts.*

Rick. Richard. My Ricky.

I will forever cherish Richard's love for Frank Sinatra. He often sang the song "My Way," and that truly describes the way he lived his life. As his wife, I complained that everything was his way, but this quality was also what I loved about him. When I'm at a loss and searching for the words to explain how everything happened, I can close my eyes and hear him singing, "Lisa Marie, do not shed these tears, my dear love." And he's right. He did it his way.

Questions for Reflection

1. What are the best things you can remember about the people you've lost?
2. How do they influence your life today?
3. How do you honor them on the anniversary of their death?

Chapter 17

The Promises, the End, the Defeat

Forgiveness is the fragrance
The violet sheds on the heel
That has crushed it.

—Mark Twain

Everyone has experienced some sort of loss in his or her lifetime at some level. Either the person has had a traumatic childhood experience or suffered through emotional, physical, or mental anguish due to a series of life events. Rose, Rico, and Enzo have gone through their loving parents' divorce and the death of their father. The feelings of loss that came with these events will influence their lives forever.

So many people just need to know there is someone who cares—someone who will sit and listen to their story. Their story is part of them. The grief, anger, and resentment we're holding onto need kindness if they're going to be processed. We all have a burden, and I have discovered that when we treat ourselves with kindness and love, we soften the blow. Personally, I couldn't keep all this locked up inside anymore. I refused to allow it to eat away at my gut and melt my mind, so I gave myself the kindness I needed to grieve.

When I did, I found so much beauty outside my front door—so much beautiful air to breathe. I wanted to capture it. I opened my door, and I breathed in the air. I continued on, walking my path with a spring in my step. I walked toward the thriving green forest and the stream of water glistening in the sunlight. I refused to take the path into the dark. *We are all worthy of more*, I told myself.

I am fortunate enough that I was able to pick myself off the floor, brush myself off, and get back on my own destined path in the wake of Rick's death. I know how to handle the fear of others while keeping my thoughts running straight on my path. I have learned to tune out what doesn't resonate with me while keeping myself open to learning and letting new possibilities come my way.

Remember that we are powerful beyond being. We are all from our creator. He died for us and made us the best he could. It's up to us to complete his mission, for it is this that will set us free.

I have chosen to walk through life with open eyes. Doing so revealed a whole new world around me. Everything started to flow in the right direction. I released my soul to allow the good in everything to come to me, and the restriction that held me back from my wants, needs, and desires disappeared.

There is a universe beyond us here on earth, whatever we may choose to call it. Some of us pray we might go back home to the arms of our heavenly Father and Mother Mary, while others believe we are living beyond anything we can even imagine. Whatever your beliefs may be, I know our loved ones live on in the spiritual world. They may become angels, who guide us each day and keep us safe. They may watch over us and smile down on us each time we pray for peace and comfort for them and others. I truly know and believe they exist near us in spirit form.

I have experienced some very profound events that are signs from Rick. Others have had this experience, too. He never fails to provide our daughter with a parking space at her busy university; one always seems to open up at just the right time. He sends me dimes to remind me that with time all will be well. Time on a dime. I find pennies he drops from heaven into laundry baskets of towels that don't have pockets, which give me something to smile about while folding the laundry. Butterflies and birds remind my heart that he is near, as do rays of sunshine coming down on my face on an otherwise-dreary day or the scent of a flower in the dead of winter. I don't let these moments pass me by. I will never forget his simple ways, and he will never forget us.

The most sincere, confident, stubborn man I knew would have never let a moment pass without letting me know how he felt. His proudest and most emotional moments were when our children were born. Each of them brought him to tears of joy, and each birth was a fresh new start. He never faltered or changed. As the saying goes, he certainly was a creature of habit.

I wanted to speak at his funeral, but I didn't for a variety of reasons. I have saved these final words to share about him. These are the words that best capture what he meant to me; what I didn't get to say; and what others didn't get to hear about the Richard we all knew, cherished, and adored. This is how I remember him.

The strength of his mind, his small round-tipped fingers. Sporting his cotton argyle and wearing a white Titleist cap.

After a busy work season, the skin on his delicate hands might show a few calluses.

The pride he showed in his work and the care and time he took with his customers were the same pride and affection he showed for his family.

He dreamed of the taste of a vanilla twist while wearing L. L. Bean on his wrist, driving a red Alfa Romeo Spider Pininfarina, snapping to a little bit of Sinatra., stopping to have a chat with a friend while sipping a martini with olives filled to the brim, or lighting up a cigar but never very far.

If you were lucky enough to get him off the fresh spring turf, you might have spotted him on the sixth with a view. Everyone knew he would have a three wood, complete with gold screws molded in hand ... perfection in everything, careful not to drive it into the sand. Come on, my friend, twist off with a Bud, listening to his favorite band.

His reality was the weekly "run," deeply bolting a verse of White or anything Motown, cruising town in his red Sienna while dreaming of a trip to Vienna. Chilling and grilling were his specialty for all those who stopped in to taste. Nothing ever went to waste.

His wisdom and wit kept us on our toes. One fierce look of his eyes, and you were reminded that "Papa always knows."

He had a stern, hard exterior, but in one conversation you felt his kind, marshmallow interior.

Golf balls, Bucks, and Weejuns. One firm handshake, and you'd have made a friend for life. I am blessed and grateful to have once been called his wife.

Questions for Reflection

1. How do you know your lost loved ones are still with you?
2. What choices or decisions in your life are making them proud of you?
3. How can your grief for those you have lost help you love the people who are still with you today?

Epilogue

And so,
there is always home.
We all come from somewhere.
The root of the plant had to start ...
It was a beginning.
You plant your feet on the ground, and your family roots
begin to grow.
Your path is nurtured, loved, and respected.
It's a place you can and will always come back to.
Your memories always remain, no matter where life
may take you.
Welcome home.

One night in 2014, Andrew gathered everyone around the table for a delicious pot roast dinner he had cooked. Family dinners are very important to Andrew and me; we never miss a six o'clock dinner. It is a special time for us to gather as a family and reunite after a long, hard day at work or school. It both brings us and keeps us together. Our family fills seven seats at the dining table. That night Rose, Rico, Enzo, Tilly, and Bella all joined us to hear what Andrew had to say.

This evening was particularly special, because Andrew wanted to make sure the three older children understood the promise he had made to their father. Shortly before Rick's death, Rick had had several meetings and extensive conversations with Andrew. Rick knew he was dying, and the thought of how his children would be cared for long after he was gone haunted him. He wanted to help make sure they were well educated so they could take care of themselves later in life.

We were fortunate that our children had a bond with their stepfather, yet he knew he would never take the place of their papa. What he could do was provide them with unconditional love. He promised to support their careers and life endeavors in any way possible.

And he has. Andrew and I are clear about our values, and one of them is that our life's passion is our children. Since that night at the table, we have continued to strive to help them become the best humans they can be. Although the daily task of balancing all our schedules, careers, and life ambitions can sometimes become overwhelming, we have managed to keep an open, optimistic view of the future. We choose to live without limits.

I am a very proud mama. The journey has been fulfilling. We spent a few years in the USA and are now once again returning to Europe with Enzo, Tilly, and Bella; this time we are moving to Switzerland. Four years after we sat around the table and discussed Rick's plans for Andrew and the kids, I am happy to say they are thriving.

Rose is well on her way in life. She has completed her master of science degree and is pursuing a PhD. As the eldest daughter, she continues to act as the adult nurturing mother in the family and is the confidante for others. Rico is beginning his second year of his master's degree in architecture and is a natural artist, who designs incredible pieces while bringing our family balance. His soft, positive nature keeps us laughing, and he continually inspires us to be our best. Enzo will attend his last two years of high school while living with us in Switzerland. He remains extremely independent and has grown to be a fine young man. Like my grandfather, he is a jack-of-all-trades, whose wisdom goes well beyond his years.

Tilly and Bella will be attending primary and middle school in Switzerland as well. Tilly has a sweet smile and gentle nature. Her healing hands can instantly melt away any worries your body may hold. Bella is spunky, always filled with a great riddle or two. Her artistic nature will leave you feeling like you just had a visit to Monet's garden. They both continue to strengthen their skiing skills and pursue their interests in art and fashion.

We will forever grieve the loss of Rick. And our family continues on. Powerless to our situation, we found a way to be limitless anyway.

We did it our way.

Acknowledgments

This book began with words jotted down on any paper I could find. During the dark moments, my yellow legal pads became a place of comfort. One after another, I filled the pages with hand scribbles. At nighttime, when I placed my head down on my pillow to rest, the silence of the night brought me messages, words I needed to voice. Little did I know how much my internal self was longing to heal.

On a deeply personal level, *A Limitless Life in a Powerless World* became a story that needed to be spoken.

To my coach and fantastic editor, Chandika Devi: Thank you for coaching and encouraging me to dive into the depth of what needed to heal. Here's my sincere gratitude to you for steering me through the process of embracing my powerlessness. Without your incredible patience and insightfulness, I wouldn't have been able to have my aha moments. I am forever grateful for those tear-filled breakthroughs, which led to bringing my vision into raw reality. Thank you from the bottom of my heart for allowing me to remind myself that I am limitless. It has been a true pleasure working with you and getting my heartfelt story out into the world.

To Kelly Notaras: Thank you for following your dream and creating a top-notch editing company at kn literary arts. Your matchmaker services rock! I am eternally grateful to have been matched with the best coach and editor that fit my needs. Divine timing led me to meet you in magical Maui. Had my gut instinct and intuition not brought me to you, *A Limitless Life in a Powerless World* would still be sitting on paper.

To Reid Tracy: Thank you for continuing to honor the vision of Louise Hay. My deepest gratitude to you for providing the platform aspiring writers need. The writers' workshops Hay House provides allowed me to embark on my journey and wake up the spiritual words that needed to be spoken.

To Balboa Press: Over a year ago, the first person I met at Hay House's writers' conference in Maui was Sandy Powell. I sat and admired her from afar while she carefully set up her display of brochures and pamphlets. With pride she displayed all the authors who had published their creative work. I sat in awe and whispered to myself, *I need to meet this woman.* On that day, I had no idea how the universe knew exactly how much I needed her. I kept getting a nudge to get up and walk over to her table. When I did, she encouraged me to continue with my dream and publish my book. Thank you, Sandy, for your continued support and for helping me navigate the book publishing process. Your team has been supportive and patient.

To my beloved husband Andrew: My love. Thank you for accepting the challenge of taking on the biggest department you have ever managed. Without you there would be no "us." Your love, extraordinary level of patience, and utmost strength in keeping us all together go beyond infinity. Thank you for your constant encouragement to keep going as you lead me through all these grandiose adventures. Thank you for supporting my late-night writing sessions during the past year. I love you to the moon and back, and I am eternally grateful for you.

To my daughter Rose: Thank you for believing in me, even when you didn't want to know. I will forever embrace your strength and brilliant mind. Thank you for being the nurturing older sister to your siblings.

To Rico, my boy: Thank you for inspiring me with your creative mind. Your support and encouragement to finish my writings were my beacon of light. When you finished a piece of work, I was inspired to finish a chapter. Remember, an artist's work is never done.

To Enzo, my fulfillment and my strength: Thank you for walking along this journey with us. I would be lost without you. I know that though at times we seem to be an organized mess, you are the glue that holds us together. I love you forever.

To Tilly, my sweet daughter: You are my gift that I graciously unwrap every day. My savior and intuitive gift. Thank you for always inspiring me to write, create, and dream. Thank you for your calmness, and I am most blessed for your healing hands. Always sparkle and shine.

To Bella, my fierce, compassionate girl: Your artistic ability will take you far. Your vivid imagination has kept me going along this writing journey. Thank you for always inspiring me with your amazing drawings. May you always wake up with limitless thinking.

To my parents: I am truly blessed for the life you have given me. Your continued love and support have been greatly appreciated. I am forever grateful for the life lessons you have taught me and am honored to be your daughter.

To my only sibling, my brother: Thank you for always reminding me where I was raised and for bringing me home to the right side of Transit Road.

To Julie, my savior in the night hours of writing: Thank you for always answering my call and reading my words at two a.m. Your praise for me and your swift kicks in the ass to keep writing have been instrumental on my journey. The ongoing support you give me and the reminder to keep creating my magic have been deeply appreciated.

To Jenni, my beautiful one: Thank you for jumping on our crazy train many years ago. Thank you for capturing the most incredible photos and making memories with us. I am most grateful for your "drop everything" motto because Lisa Marie needs a photo shoot. You walked along my side during this whole long process of creation, and I am most grateful. God sent me an angel, and I am truly blessed to have you in my life.

To my soul sister Deb: Thank you for always saying yes to the next adventure, even when you don't know where my crazy, wild side will take us. Thank you for sitting with me through multiple double feature movies so I could get my writing mode on. Trains, planes, and automobiles—we have done it all. Boats included. You are my constant and the only one who can keep me grounded when I need it. Thank you from the depths of my soul for supporting my story of healing.

I am deeply grateful for the special people in my life who have encouraged me on my quest to get this book published. You have impacted my life this past year in profound ways, even if it was just a smile in passing, an act of kindness, or a word of love. You made me feel like I was never alone in my writing journey. Special thanks to Dawn Lynn Greyson, Dede Hart, Owen Ortolani, Sandra Rein, Mrs. Pattie Rich, Tracy Hansberger Chocol, and Shelby Wilde.

To God: Thank you for loving me endlessly. Thank you for always answering me when I call.

And lastly, I thank you, my readers. I am grateful to share my memoir with you and hope you are able to get unstuck and live your life limitlessly.

Printed and bound by PG in the USA